Bold Girls Speak

Bold Girls Speak

Girls of the Bible Come Alive Today

MARY STROMER HANSON

Illustrated by
LISA GUINTHER

WIPF & STOCK · Eugene, Oregon

BOLD GIRLS SPEAK
Girls of the Bible Come Alive Today

Copyright © 2013 Mary Stromer Hanson. All rights reserved. Except for brief quotations in critical publications or reviews, no part of this book may be reproduced in any manner without prior written permission from the publisher. Write: Permissions. Wipf and Stock Publishers, 199 W. 8th Ave., Suite 3, Eugene, OR 97401.

Wipf & Stock
An Imprint of Wipf and Stock Publishers
199 W. 8th Ave., Suite 3
Eugene, OR 97401

www.wipfandstock.com

ISBN 13: 978-1-62032-482-0

Manufactured in the U.S.A.

Dedicated to
Rev. Jonathan D. Male
1935–1996
"I will sing of the mercies of the Lord forever"

Contents

Foreword / ix
Acknowledgments / xi

Miriam Who Negotiated: Exodus 2 / 1

Five Sisters Who Asked for Their Inheritance:
  Numbers 27:1–11; Joshua 17:3–6 / 18

The Girl Who Spied: 2 Samuel 14; 2 Samuel 17:17 / 35

The Servant Girl Who Boldly Witnessed: 2 Kings 5 / 51

The Daughters Who Built the Walls of Jerusalem: Nehemiah 3:12 / 67

The Girl Whose Hand Jesus Touched:
  Matthew 9:18–25; Mark 5:21–43; Luke 8:40–56 / 84

The Maids Who Questioned: Matthew 26:69–75; Mark 14:66–72;
  Luke 22:54–62; John 18:15–27 / 102

Rhoda, the Servant Girl Who Persisted: Acts 12:5–17 / 120

The Girl Who Found Her Own Voice: Acts 16:16–40 / 138

The Daughters Who Prophesied: Acts 21:8; Acts 23:35 / 153

Lesson Plan Ideas / 173
Matching Quiz / 175
Quiz Your Knowledge of Bold Girls Speak / 176
The Maids Who Questioned: Stage Play Version / 178

Foreword

I WAS LISTENING TO a sermon titled the "Raising of the Daughter of Jairus," sometime in the mid-1990s, when it occurred to me that I wished I had noticed that passage when I was much younger. Normally, Mark 5:21–43 is taught from the point of view of the father, or Jesus, or the disciples, but I wondered why not give attention to the girl's experience? This daughter was precious in the sight of both her parents and Jesus. Throughout my childhood Christian education, I had the impression that girls were invisible in the church. The stories were always about the men, kings, disciples, and some sons. Occasionally a woman would show up, but never a girl. I realized how empowering it could be for girls to see themselves in the Bible stories. I quickly thought of a few more girls who are under-represented in the Sunday school lesson books. Since then, I have discovered even more girls tucked into overlooked verses, both in the Old and New Testament.

Throughout years of teaching school and then in seminary training, I never let go of the idea of developing these stories. It must have been a calling; I rewrote them many times as I gained more knowledge and experience as a writer. The ten stories in this book are written as accurately as possible to their historical, cultural, and biblical settings. To enrich the learning possibilities of these stories, I have created additional episodes that bring in more female characters and experiences. These girls are brave and smart. They make the best of difficult situations, often in foreign cultures and under the condition of forced servitude. They solve problems and survive, all the while witnessing to their faith and living true to their God. The stories in this book can be read in chronological order, but doing so is not necessary because each story is self-contained. Although girls are the main characters in these stories, most include boys as well. This book can be used for classes or for individual enjoyment. Depending on the discretion of teachers and parents, more mature students can be guided through a discussion of the suggested questions that follow each story. The stories themselves are appropriate for any audience.

The pastor who I listened to that Sunday morning so long ago was Rev. Jonathan D. Male (1935–1996) of Park Hill Presbyterian Church in Denver, Colorado. He was a kind and generous man who encouraged and helped me heal during a hard time in my life. A few short years later, he met his maker on Christmas Eve, a victim of cancer that took his life too early. His inspiration and encouragement caused me to begin writing these stories, and it is in his memory I dedicate this book.

Acknowledgments

MANY PEOPLE HAVE HELPED me complete the writing of this book, which spanned more than a decade. Before I started seminary, several good friends read my first attempts at writing stories. Merry and Linda Male read my early tentative efforts. Mary Ellen Sweeny, PhD, applied her editing skills to an early draft. I also attended the Colorado Christian Writers Conferences at Estes Park and Mt. Hermon where I benefited from Tricia Goyer's fiction writers workshop. Outstanding English teachers, Margaret Wehner and Colette Schneider (1946–2012), from the Montview Presbyterian Church, Denver, and Patty Crowley from "316" helpfully read through manuscripts.

I owe many thanks to the professors of Denver Seminary whose classes greatly added to my background knowledge and writing ability. Dr. Richard Hess reviewed the Old Testament stories; Dr. Judith Diehl edited the New Testament stories, and Dr. Hélène Dallaire reviewed the New Testament stories with an eye toward Second Temple Jewish background. They greatly increased my confidence that the historical, cultural, and theological background is as accurate as possible. Rev. Dr. Richard Craft read over one of my last drafts, reading from beginning to end. My collaboration with Lisa Guinther, who also read everything with a philosopher's point of view, adds the visual appeal to the book as the illustrator. I thank her for her prayer support and enthusiasm for the project.

Last, but not least, I thank the members of the Denver Seminary writers' group who read all the stories and corrected many mistakes, great and minute. This group includes Peggy McIntyre, MA; Megan Jooranstad, MA; Grace Kong, M Div; and Jean Hess D Min. My greatest thanks and love to my husband, Clement, and children, Ben and Anne, none of who have read any of this, but nevertheless indulge Mom in her study and writing passion.

Miriam Who Negotiated
Exodus 2

THE HARDSHIP BECOMES HARDER

WITH EVERY STEP SHE slogged through the mud, water splashed from the baskets swinging from a wooden yoke across her shoulders. She and many other children had run the path countless times, which became swampier as the day wore on. They ran to the river, a tributary of the Nile, scooped up water, and carried it to the vats where workers raked the clay and straw into a thick mud. Their tightly woven baskets, lined with pitch, did not hold up under the constant hard use.

"Faster, you Hebrew slaves, you sluggards," the slave master commanded while he cracked his whip near her heels. The children could not keep up with the brick makers' demand for water. All afternoon she had run to the river, filled her container, and then carried it as fast as she could to the tubs. Her back hurt, her hands were cramped, and her legs were rubbed raw by the rough baskets.

"You dogs, you filthy lazy Hebrews, faster; Pharaoh will cancel your next day of rest if the quota is not reached." Another slave driver cracked a whip over the workers at the tubs. They were so used to it they did not even flinch at the sound.

Every drop of water was necessary, yet she and the other children could only carry so much. The basket was watertight that morning, but it would start to leak from the creases as the day wore on. When the leaking became impossible, she had to use clay jars, and they were much heavier. If she did not get enough water to the brick makers, the Egyptian taskmasters would whip the workers who were her kinsfolk, her father and mother, extended family, and many villagers.

Wooden frames lay on the ground that formed hundreds of rectangles. Workers poured the mud into each of the molds and leveled off the top smoothly. The mud soon firmed up, and then the frame could be carefully lifted off to reveal new bricks, which would bake in the sun. The number of rows times the number of bricks in each row was carefully counted, and represented the total day's work for Miriam's village. At sunset, the Egyptian overseer would come over and note the final tally. If the number was not high enough, harsh words and penalties would be shouted.

"Pharaoh already has a huge palace. I would like to do some building on my own house," one Hebrew worker said to another.

"How many children does he have?" another Hebrew asked. "He is said to have numerous princesses and princes. You can see them playing in the gardens. One princess even collects wounded animals and has a sort of menagerie," someone added.

"His heart is as dead as those mummies they bury, all dried out. He certainly doesn't care about our homes and children," the Hebrews complained among themselves. "How can we keep building for him when he treats us like mere animals?"

The climate was cooler in the eastern edge of the Nile delta where Pharaoh was adding rooms to his already magnificent summer residence. When the new bricks were hard as stone, they were carried to the building site. As the walls grew higher, many columns and brightly painted murals were added to the building. Some of the Hebrew slaves were skilled in special techniques for crafting tiles and monuments. All of the workers for

Miriam Who Negotiated

this project lived in a village especially built for them, just out of view of the palace, because after all, Pharaoh did not want the Hebrews as close neighbors. He only valued their hard labor.

Finally, the sun dipped behind the bluffs in the west and the work day came to an end. Miriam straightened her back and stretched her hands, which were callused from the carrying. She spied her brother, Aaron, in the distance. They reconnected with their parents and prepared for the short walk back to their village.

The weary family members greeted each other with a hug, "Miriam and Aaron, another day is safely over, how are you?" Their mother, Jochebed asked as she hugged her children together. They moved to gather their water flasks and bags that held their meager lunches from under a shrub, where they had hidden them at noon, the last time they saw each other.

"How good it will be to get home," their father Amram said while throwing a bag over his back. "Praise to the God of Abraham, let's get back." His steps toward the village were interrupted by a shout from the worksite.

"We can't go yet, the bosses have to talk to us," an uncle called in their direction.

"This is never good news, what can it be now," Jochebed groaned.

The workers gathered around an Egyptian governor who shouted at them.

"You Hebrews are becoming too strong," the Egyptian governor said. He stood on a stone block that towered over the sweat-soaked workers. "We will cut you down to size. You are foreigners here; you are meant to be slaves, and slaves you will remain. Recently you have become proud. Frankly, we Egyptians were getting a little fearful of you. Things always seem to go well with you. Your god blesses you, but that will stop; we are greater. Our Pharaoh is greater than your god. The old government favored you, but now things are changing. We will see to that. Starting now, life will become much harder for you. Before you worked your short hours, now the workdays will be longer with fewer days off. From now on, it will be harder for you to survive; one way or another, your numbers will decrease."

The Hebrew slaves stood motionless in their fatigue, scarcely believing their ears. Only a gentle evening breeze stirred through the work site, slightly drying the sweat on their brows.

The mood was subdued as the family walked home. "How can they expect us to do more?" the children asked.

"How long will the God of our ancestors remain silent?" Amram asked. "What do they mean we will become fewer in number? Our father, Abraham was promised we Hebrews would become a great nation and as numerous as the stars."

"Doesn't he see our suffering?" Jochebed answered. "Will he ever send relief? Why do we only have questions and never any answers?"

GOOD NEWS BECOMES BAD

Their clay brick house was located in a crowded village. The houses were closely packed together, side-by-side, with common walls separating the families of construction workers. This village had been quickly built several years back when construction on this palace was started. Most evenings and nights were hot, so the families slept under a canopy on the roof. Conversation carried easily along the roofs and through the opened windows between the neighbors, so the workers talked in hushed tones. The elders, who told us stories of Hebrew history, recalled that Joseph and his descendants first settled in the lush green area of the Nile delta in a city called Rameses where their flocks had good grazing for many generations. When new Egyptian rulers no longer remembered the promises made to Joseph, the Hebrews lost their freedom. Now they had to work as slaves and were forced to move close to the building sites and live in hastily built houses. But these flimsy structures had become permanent homes. Miriam could not remember the place where she was born. Her parents often said that they were blessed to be together as a family. Sometimes the men had to leave their families for long periods of time to go to another construction site.

One day, Miriam returned to her house after fetching water for their household. In the oppressive noonday heat, the crowded village was strangely quiet. Babies did not seem to cry anymore and neighborhood conversation had become much less trusting. Her mother was drying her eyes in her father's rough work tunic, and he had draped his arms across her shoulders. Miriam felt awkward when she interrupted their embrace.

"Don't go away, we have something important to tell you," they reassured Miriam when she started to back out of the room. "A baby will soon be born in our family." Miriam's first reaction was to shout out with excitement, but her shriek of joy was stifled when her mother hugged her close. She was puzzled when her parents so quickly hushed her up.

Miriam Who Negotiated

"But why can't I shout out with joy about another child?" Miriam pleaded.

"The Egyptians are planning still more burdens for us to bear. This is a dreadful time to have a newborn baby in Egypt," her parents whispered to her. "Life for the Hebrews is hard enough without an infant. If the baby is a girl, she might survive, but if it is a boy . . ." They were unable to finish the sentence. Her mother held back a sob.

"If it is a boy . . . what did they mean by this?" Miriam puzzled over her parents' remark. The only children in their family were her brother, Aaron, and she. They were close together in age and almost past childhood.

Miriam and Aaron later discussed the situation between themselves.

"A baby in the family would be fun. Most of the Hebrew families are much larger than ours," Aaron said. They considered their family as contented as Hebrews could be in Egypt, considering the misery of their surroundings.

"Well, how did this happen? If our parents know it is dangerous to get a baby at this time, can't they delay it coming?" Aaron asked Miriam. His slightly older sister always had answers to tough questions.

"Aaron, do I have to explain everything to you?" Miriam snapped back. She sighed to herself. It must have happened at the time of a spring festival. Now it was late summer; the baby would be born in the hardest time of the year, the winter. In addition, her mother was not young anymore and worn out from all the work.

Their parents frequently reminded them, "The God of our fathers, Abraham, Isaac, and Jacob, has blessed us and saved us from famine. He will save us from the Egyptians as well."

Miriam started doing more of the errands outside the house so her mother could stay hidden inside. Her parents became increasingly anxious as her mother's abdomen became more round.

"It is very important that you do not talk to anyone about a baby being born to our house," their father repeated to them often. "Especially the Egyptians must not know, and they have spies all over. We must all try to do still more work at the worksite so Mother is not missed."

"But, why not tell our friends and neighbors? Can't they know?" She felt like her parents were trying to protect her from something.

"It will prevent awkward questions later," was all their father would say. They obeyed him carefully, but Miriam wondered. She made many trips to the river to do washing. Because of the time spent doing daily errands to help her mother, she was spending more time with other village women.

One day Miriam learned the dreadful details about the latest command of Pharaoh. At the river, two Hebrew women were stooped over the water, appearing to wash clothes, but their attention was totally focused on their conversation.

"What more can they do to us, Puah?" One deeply tanned woman complained to the other. "The workers already have to make endless bricks for Pharaoh's monuments in this baking sun. In addition, they keep increasing the fieldwork, and yet the Egyptians are never satisfied. The cruel slave masters threaten the workers every minute with a whipping if bricks aren't made fast enough," she continued.

"Shiphrah, we cannot even help the women anymore with labor and delivery," said the other women. "Pharaoh has noticed that Hebrew boy babies survive even though he commanded us Hebrew midwives to kill the newborn baby boys."

"Of course, I, along with you my dear friend, could not ever kill any babies, Egyptian or Hebrew, Puah said. I have even attended Egyptian mothers when they give birth, and it would have been easy enough to suffocate a newborn. Just hold a hand over the baby's mouth and nose slightly longer than necessary when clearing the airway, or turn their face under water during their first bath. Not even the mother suspects that the baby wasn't stillborn."

"If I couldn't do that to even an Egyptian baby, I certainly couldn't suffocate the children of my kinfolk. That would be just like the crocodile from the Nile lying in wait to devour the baby as soon as it takes the first breath," Shiphrah shuddered at the thought. "No, in the eyes of the great God of Abraham, that is not what we do."

"Well we told Pharaoh's messengers that the Hebrew mothers give birth quickly without any help," continued Puah. "And that is almost true, most of the time. But now we can't be seen near a residence with a pregnant woman or the Egyptians will suspect that a birth occurred."

"Any Egyptian has permission to spy and kill any baby boy they find," Shiphrah moaned.

"Only the boy babies are to be killed; what are they thinking?" asked Puah.

Miriam Who Negotiated

"Oh don't think they are being merciful by saving the girls. They want the girl babies to grow up and be used as slaves for their own evil purposes," whispered Shiphrah.

"What can we do to save the babies?" asked Puah. "Can the mothers be smuggled to a secret hiding place until delivery and the boy babies raised safely away from Egypt?"

Miriam silently turned toward home and felt her heart sink. "Now I understand!" she exclaimed to herself. But other questions immediately came to her. "What if our new baby is a boy? Why do they hate us so much?"

Later her mother reassured her. "The God of Abraham has brought us through hard times before. He is always faithful to protect his people. We are his chosen people, and he will show us a way to survive," she said.

Winter arrived, it was colder, and they had blankets over the windows. "So, if the baby is a girl, it is safe. But if it is a boy and the Egyptians find him, they will throw him into the river?" Aaron asked.

"Our God of the Hebrews determines if we have a boy or a girl. We will persevere," Amram reminded them. "Even the circumcision ceremonies have been dropped, although this has been the custom since Abraham," he added. "If the baby is a girl, we will also keep it secret to help protect those parents who have boys," her mother added. "If no one is sure if the baby is a boy or girl, then no one is responsible to report to the authorities. Of course it is best to keep the baby as secret as possible. Spies are all over."

"A midwife cannot be seen coming to our house to help with the delivery," Miriam repeated.

"No, Jochebed, don't think about that," Amram said. He hugged his wife. "I won't let you have the baby alone."

A BABY IS BORN, BUT WILL HE LIVE?

After months of fearful waiting, the worst happened! It was a moonless winter night when a healthy baby boy was born.

"As they say about the Hebrew women, they give birth easily," her father said. "The God of our ancestors is blessing us, even in this hardship. We will find a way of keeping this son alive."

Now Miriam's family had a new baby brother, at least for now. Miriam helped her mother with the infant for the first months, anticipating his every need. He seldom cried, and he was not discovered by the Egyptians.

Miriam grew to love her brother very much, but he was becoming more active.

"We won't be able to hide the baby much longer," Miriam's mother said one day.

"Mother, I cannot bear the thought of my baby brother dying," Miriam sighed. Her arms automatically crossed in front of her to make a rocking motion. "What can we do to save him?" pleaded Miriam.

"We will not give up and let the Egyptians destroy us," her mother said. She clenched her fists and added, "Our God will help us find a way to save the baby."

Miriam started thinking as she wandered past the point where the Hebrews did their washing. She ventured dangerously close to the beach that was off-limits to the Hebrews. There, she noticed an Egyptian princess bathing with her attendants. "I wonder if she is the one that collects wounded animals. If she would only care for the Hebrew babies as much as she does ducks and wild kittens."

The partially finished palace towered beyond. It featured brightly colored columns and was covered in many fanciful designs. Lotus flowers and water lilies decorated the upper edges of the roof, which was supported by columns of drawings of many animals such as jackals, lions, and snakes. An abundance of birds such as owls, falcons, and ducks seemed so real that they could take wing and fly away. The symbols could be read by some people, but she was told they mostly expressed how great Pharaoh was as king and god. The giant eyes really troubled her; they seemed to look right at her. They symbolized the eye of Horus, one of the Egyptian gods. The Egyptians believed the eyes could see everything. If this was true, why didn't their god see the evil caused by Pharaoh?

The God of the Hebrews also promised Abraham that the Hebrews would have their own land where they would rule and not be ruled, and he also saw everything.

What was happening to the baby boys? Her heart was crushed to think about it. Were they being devoured by crocodiles? Yet she had not heard of any being killed. Were they being sent somewhere? How could her brother be saved?

Miriam returned home. She and her mother quietly started to work out a plan.

"Can we make something waterproof, yet lightweight?" Miriam pondered.

"A clay jar won't leak, but it also won't float. A basket will float for a short time, but eventually becomes waterlogged and sinks," her mother thought aloud.

"We need the pitch that drains from wood when it is burnt. Tree sap drips out into a basin under the fire as the wood turns into charcoal. Egypt does not have many trees, so where can we find wood to burn. Where do the workers get the pitch that lines the baskets we use to carry water?" Miriam asked. "Father and Aaron will try to get some from the work site."

Miriam and her mother worked on the problem of building a waterproof basket for many weeks. Miriam gathered the toughest papyrus stalks from the riverbanks, and her mother expertly wove a basket. Their hearts grew heavier with every passing day, as the danger to the baby boy grew greater.

"Have we made the basket skillfully enough that it will not leak?" Miriam wondered. She took it to the river filled with clothes to wash. It floated like a boat when she tested it.

"Do we dare hope that the princess will have pity for a Hebrew baby and rescue him?" The family anguished over the question.

It was summer when Jochebed hugged her baby boy, knowing it was the last time. The most she dared to hope is that he would live, somewhere, somehow. If only he would be permitted to grow up in the company of others. Would another mother raise him, perhaps love him? Miriam kissed her baby brother before they wrapped him snugly and placed him in the little ark. Her mother was shaking with violent sobs when Miriam left the house, yet no sound could be heard. Her father and Aaron had left their last kisses that morning. They absolutely could not be missed at the work site.

Miriam then gently carried him to the river, pretending as though the basket contained clothes to wash. She checked to be sure there were no crocodile tracks in the sand and set the basket afloat near the beach where Pharaoh's daughter usually bathed. She shuddered deeply and gave the basket a determined push. The little ark lightly drifted away in the current.

Miriam thought her pounding heart would fail. She remembered what her mother said, "Only trust in God that he will protect the baby and will give you strength to carry him to the river."

Tall reeds rattled in the hot breeze blowing off the mighty Nile River. Keeping herself hidden, she crouched at the shore and peered over the sparkling water. Little frogs and an abundance of crickets scampered around her feet, and she was startled when a giant crane lifted gracefully into the sky. This beach was off-limits to her, for she was within sight of the white columns of the summer palace complex of Pharaoh. She had heard about amazing monuments just beyond the western horizon. There was a sphinx that looked like a crouching lion with a human face, and there were pyramids made entirely of huge stone blocks that took many humans to move. They were the tallest structures to be seen anywhere where people lived, so she had heard, and they were actually tombs of past kings. These structures were already ancient when her ancestor, Joseph, and his brothers came here to escape famine. About four hundred years ago, the Hebrews were honored guests, actually invited by the pharaoh, to seek refuge from a famine that was devastating their country. Now it had come to the tragedy she was personally facing. "Dear God of our ancestors, what happened to your promises to Abraham?" she prayed to herself.

Miriam nervously parted the reeds to improve her view when, as expected in the midmorning, several young women approached the riverbank. They chattered with carefree ease as they loosened their sandals. Cool mud squeezed between her toes when Miriam shifted to remain out of sight. Some of the maids threw stones in the water to see if any crocodiles would rise to the surface. Then they gathered up their gauzy, white gowns and waded in to be certain the water was clear of the reptiles. If the waters were safe, then the princess herself could start to bathe. Miriam's eyes were riveted on the fragile-looking basket that was gently bobbing in the waves.

"Will they see it? Then what will they do?" Miriam whispered under her breath. She watched a regal young Egyptian woman approach the water, obviously the princess. The princess casually shook off her fine sandals and threw them into a heap with the others. Running toward the water, she tucked her white linen gown into her belt to free her legs and hands for movement. Miriam noticed that the young attendants were not much older than she herself was, yet they seemed to come from a different world. Their legs were creamy white and unmarred by the scratches and bruises that Miriam acquired in the hard work of her daily existence. The tallest woman, the princess, was always the center of attention. The maids swam around her adoringly and made her laugh with their antics in the water. Could this princess be aware of the cruel suffering that occurred in the shadows of her luxurious life?

Miriam and the Hebrew girls also swam in the Nile waters but on a different beach, where the sand was not so fine. Still, in another time and place, Miriam felt these young women could have been her friends.

Miriam Who Negotiated

Abruptly, the playful movement stopped as one in the group spied the basket bobbing in the waves. They raised their hands to shield their eyes against the glaring sunlight for a better view.

Miriam's family had anticipated this moment for weeks. They had prepared and prayed; no other idea occurred to them except to take this chance to assure survival of their baby. The life of her baby brother was now in the hands of this young princess. Would she take pity and save this precious small life? Miriam froze and silently prayed, "Please God, please..."

MIRIAM SPEAKS, GOD SAVES

Miriam moved closer to the shore of the Nile, protectively watching over the ark. Silence fell over the water when the princess and her maids all looked curiously over at the basket.

"Wade over toward the reeds and bring me that quaint little basket," the princess asked one of her servants. "Do I hear a baby cry?"

An attendant waded quickly over to retrieve the basket before it drifted farther away. Miriam clasped her hands together in front of her face and hardly dared to look while the maids gathered around the princess. She carefully lifted the lid off the basket. The group of women gasped with surprise.

"Look, it is a boy baby; surely one of the Hebrews' children," she exclaimed as she lifted him out. "He is crying! Even though my father has demanded that all Hebrew baby boys should be killed, this is a beautiful child whom I want to keep and raise as my own."

Miriam's heart pounded with joy at hearing those words. God had indeed been merciful! Then she impulsively did something that was not a part of the plan. Without thinking, she stepped into the water and approached the princess. She had to make the move immediately. After all, the baby was crying, what else was she supposed to do?

Miriam bravely approached the princess. "Shall I go and choose a nurse for you from among the Hebrew women, that she may care for the baby?" Miriam asked. "Yes, go and do that," said the Egyptian princess.

It was that simple! If ever the hand of the great God of Abraham was visible, it was now!

Miriam shook uncontrollably as she ran back to the house. "Of course mother won't believe this news immediately. I will have to drag her back to the river, and quickly, before the princess changes her mind," Miriam thought aloud.

"Mother, Mother, dry your eyes," Miriam sobbed with joy. She tried to stay as calm as she could. "Come with me immediately, but don't let the princess know that the baby is yours."

They hastened to the river where the princess and her attendants stood in a circle around the baby, cooing with admiration and suggesting names.

"Here is a Hebrew woman who has her own baby. She would be glad to nurse this baby as well." Miriam tried to keep her voice calm and somewhat disinterested.

"Take this baby and nurse him for me, and I will pay you." The princess cast an approving eye at the breasts of Miriam's mother, who did not dare stammer a word. "His name is Moses because I drew him out of the water."

"Oh, his name is Moses?" Miriam almost gave herself away. Her family had been calling him by another name; but never mind, any name would be wonderful. "Yes, Moses is an appropriate name," she quickly recovered. Miriam's mother took her baby, now called Moses, into her arms and managed a slight smile. She unfastened her robe in front and started to nurse

Miriam Who Negotiated

him on their walk home from the river; her breasts were overflowing by this time.

The baby's own mother would be taking care of him as before! Miriam could not wait to tell Aaron and her father. She thought of her first song at this time as she joyfully sang praises to God that the plan had been successful. In this clever way, with the blessing of the God of Abraham, Miriam managed to save her brother as well as reunite him with her family! The princess even paid the mother wages to take care of her own baby!

Now the family could stay together for a few more years. When Moses was older, he began to live in Pharaoh's household as an Egyptian son, and there he enjoyed all the privileges of a young prince. He was educated to become an Egyptian ruler, learning their language and customs, but he never forgot who he was and his origin. He did not forget the God of the Hebrews. We will hear from Moses and Miriam again!

POINTS TO PONDER ABOUT MIRIAM

Girls and boys have a marvelous gift, characteristic of children of all lands and all ages. How many times have you taken pity on a living creature in need?

Both Miriam and the Egyptian princess, although they were so different, they were also so much alike. They both loved a helpless baby and wanted to save it. Girls have forever picked up and nursed the injured. This is a wonderful quality. It is sad when God's creatures are harmed, because all living things are precious in his sight. Through these daughters, one rich and one poor, God cared for the unborn baby, Moses. He cares for all life, big and small.

This *Bold Girl* showed bravery and initiative in saving her little brother. What if Miriam had been too afraid to speak to Pharaoh's daughter? This young princess was, after all, the daughter of a very powerful and cruel king. Miriam kept her secret safe as she approached the princess. She never revealed the plan to volunteer her own mother to nurse her little brother! We do not know if this was Miriam's own idea or if her family had worked it out together, but it could have turned out disastrously if she didn't proceed with complete confidence. What would have been the result if she had talked too much and told the princess the details of the plan? If she had not spoken the exact right words, Pharaoh's daughter could have decided against saving the baby Moses. Miriam changed the whole course of the history of the Israelites in Egypt by her bravery and clear thinking.

In this remarkable manner, God protected the life of Moses by Miriam's bold action. She used her brain to think of a solution. She used her mouth to speak up; yet she knew how to keep a secret. She negotiated a way to save her brother and have her mother care for her own child. What a gift it is to learn to be silent at the appropriate times, but also speak up when the time is right!

Like so many other girls throughout the ages, Miriam was happy to have a new baby in the household. This was a big step for her because now she was old enough to help care for an infant. This was the normal expectation for girls at this time and the only example they knew from the generations before them. They learned from their mothers how to take care of children and the home. Their families arranged a marriage for them in their teens and they became mothers themselves. At this time and place in history, girls could not consider school or a choice of careers. Miriam was happy to step into the challenge of being a big sister. However, her life as an adult, which can be read in the remainder of the book of Exodus and Numbers, will turn out much differently than expected for a woman at this time in history.

Be sure to compare the story of Miriam in this book with its biblical account. You can discover which parts here are fictional and which are taken directly from the Bible. You will notice that the fictional parts of Miriam's story in this book accurately depict how life was lived in Egypt at about 1200 bc. Life in ancient Egypt is a very fascinating subject to study. You can find books with many pictures, maps, and timelines. Or, better yet, make your own. Many museums have artifacts from Egypt including mummies, objects of gold, and objects taken from tombs. Maybe someday you can visit Egypt, and if you go there remember Miriam!

Miriam and her extended family, all the Hebrews, did not feel at home in Egypt, although they had never lived in another land. How many people throughout the ages and in all parts of the world have experienced this hardship? Often families have voluntarily left their familiar surroundings and moved with much expense and danger to a new place that promises more opportunity. Many people have been forced to leave their country because of invasion by foreign troops or natural disaster. Giving up a home is difficult for everyone. People with different colored skin, who speak foreign languages, worship in different ways, and prepare pungent smelling

Miriam Who Negotiated

foods have seldom been welcomed in a new land. Immigrants remember their home and do not want their children to forget the ways of the old country. In their new home, they are among strangers. They may not be well accepted and they do not understand all the new customs. Miriam lived under these conditions as well. Even though she and her family had always known Egypt as their home, it was not their homeland.

About eighty years after the story of his remarkable birth, Moses became a great leader of the Children of Israel. Times did not get easier for the Hebrews in Egypt. Moses, along with Aaron and Miriam, led their people out of the slavery they so long endured and took them to the Promised Land. You can read these exciting stories about the escape of the Israelites from Egypt through the Red Sea in the Old Testament books of Exodus and Numbers.

Miriam is a unique girl in the Bible because we meet her twice. First we meet her in this childhood scene with her baby brother Moses. We meet her again as a woman in the book of Exodus, where her story continues. When the Children of Israel cross the Red Sea (15:20–21) and wander in the wilderness for forty years, Miriam plays an active role. In the course of the history of God's people, she becomes a decisive, authoritative woman. Sometimes her leadership got her into trouble. Controversy will be her lifelong companion (Num 12:1–16). Anyone who is determined to make a difference takes this risk, and risk requires courage. Long after Miriam died, the Old Testament writer, Micah, called her a prophet along with her brothers, Aaron and Moses (Mic 6:8).

QUESTIONS FOR DISCUSSION

1. The king of Egypt had ordered all the boy babies of the Hebrews to be killed. Yet the daughter of the king rescued this particular baby who she recognized as being a son of the Hebrews. Was she being disobedient to her father?

2. Look up and read this story in the book of Exodus (Exod 2:1–10). How many different women were important in saving Moses' life? What do we know about Jochebed, the mother of Moses? (See Exod 2:1–9; 6:20: Num 26:59.) How and where did Moses find a wife? (See Exod 2:21–22; 4:20, 24–26; 18:2–6.)

3. Miriam became famous for leading the Children of Israel in singing and dancing. One of her songs is written in the Bible (Exod 15:21). What is the occasion for this song? How is music important in your worship? How can you participate and use your musical gifts?

4. Who are the Children of Israel? Who was Israel and what was his other name? How and why did Joseph go to Egypt? Be sure to familiarize yourself with the Old Testament stories that occur throughout the book of Genesis that lead the Israelites to living in Egypt.

5. Why are the Israelites going to a Promised Land? What was the promise made to Abraham?

RELATED CULTURAL AND HISTORICAL QUESTIONS TO EXPLORE

1. With background knowledge about ancient Egypt, describe and discuss how your life in the twenty-first century would compare with that of a poor girl like Miriam, or a rich girl like the Pharaoh's daughter living in ancient times.

2. Do you know about, or are you a member of, a group of people who are a cultural minority in this country? What can you do to share your culture with others, and how can you help those who are different be welcomed in church, school, and neighborhood? The Hebrews did not feel welcome in the foreign land of Egypt and were persecuted. Is this the last time this has happened in the history of the world? Why do people often feel threatened by those who are different?

3. Why were all the boy babies ordered to be killed instead of the girls, or why not both? (See Exod 1:8–10.)

4. What things can you do now or learn to do in the future that will help heal and comfort those in need?

5. Daughters and sons are mentioned in Exodus 3:22. Why are the children mentioned as the Israelites were leaving Egypt?

SUGGESTED TOPICS OF DISCUSSION FOR TEACHERS AND PARENTS OF OLDER STUDENTS

1. This lesson would provide the opportunity to discuss abortion and infanticide of unwanted babies. Are babies killed today because they are not the preferred sex, untimely, or deformed?

2. How have childbirth practices changed over the years?

3. Unfortunately, the evil of slavery has existed in most times and places throughout the history of the world. You can find additional information about the history of slavery. In ancient times, captives from wars were often made slaves of the conquering nation. Is slavery still practiced today? What people are vulnerable to being made slaves? Inform yourselves about the issue of human trafficking which is being practiced today in all parts of the world.

4. This chapter offers the opportunity to discuss circumcision: the practice, the history, and the purpose.

5. Child labor has been a reality for most of the history of the earth. Where are children still forced into hard labor today? When did laws first appear to prevent this abuse of children?

6. Is there a division of labor in the country where you now live based on nationality of workers?

7. If students are interested in archaeology, many resources are currently available to increase background knowledge, and every year more discoveries are made. The Hebrews occupied a large city called Tell el-Dab'a, which is the Rameses written of in Exodus 1:11. On modern maps, it is found in the eastern edge of the Nile delta at Avaris. A workers village has not been found at this location, but this story draws from information about a workers village at Deir el-Medina across the Nile, which is from about the same time period.

Five Sisters Who Asked for Their Inheritance

Numbers 27:1–11; Joshua 17:3–6

ALONE IN THE WILDERNESS

We huddled together in the frigid desert, staring into our meager fire. What a sight we were, the five daughters of Zelophehad—Mahlah, Noah, Hoglah, Milcah, and Tirzah—sunken in deep, silent sorrow. Many dozens of small lights surrounded us far into the horizon, each warming a family, some of them laughing together.

Tirzah, the youngest sister, interrupted our thoughts. "I don't even remember mother anymore. Now father's memory is also fading away, and we buried him only a few days ago."

"The older generation is almost all gone now including Miriam and Aaron." said Mahlah, the oldest, and the sister who reminded us of the traditions. "We are the new Children of Israel."

"Daughters, forty years ago, it seems like yesterday," we could remember Father's words. "Moses sent spies into the land of Canaan, the Promised Land. They returned carrying a huge cluster of grapes, but reported that giant people, whom we would never be able to conquer, inhabited the land. We were all afraid, except for Caleb and Joshua." At this point in the story Father always sighed. "Because of our lack of trust, God said all people twenty years or older will die in the desert and not see the Promised Land. That was the reason God declared we would wander in this wilderness for forty years." Father's words remained with us.

"I can see the fire hovering in the sky above the Tent of the Tabernacle. That means we will be setting out again in the morning. We will also leave our father's grave site," observed Hoglah, the realist among us. "Yahweh, have mercy on us! What does the future hold?" The last remark struck our hearts cold, and again we were gripped with sorrow.

A fire by night that hovered over the Ark of the Covenant, or a cloud by day, was the sign of Yahweh's leadership of the Children of Israel through the wilderness. A life of wandering was all we sisters have known, a life of nomads because we were all born in the wilderness. We could not imagine staying in a place long enough to plant a tree or a vine and see it grow to produce fruit.

The blast of trumpets woke us the next morning. "Pack up quickly, we are moving on toward the Jordan River," men shouted at us. Without our father, they think we can be bossed around.

"All this talk about the Promised Land," we complained among ourselves as we painfully got onto our feet. "We have only heard rumors our entire lives. Will we ever finally stop wandering?"

One of us gathered the fresh growth of manna that miraculously fell like rain every night around the camp. The little white flakes of vegetation were fresh and sweet every morning. "How many more ways can we cook manna?" Noah asked. "Remember the time we ate our fill of meat when flocks of partridge suddenly blew in from the west?"

"Now stop the complaining," Mahlah warned. "It never brings any good."

"Oh, yes, remember the snakes. The people complained, and they wished to have stayed in Egypt," said Milcah who was not fond of snakes. "We know what Father told us about Egypt. He was still a boy during the Exodus, but he remembered the terrible times when the Israelites were captives. The Egyptians were cruel slave masters."

"Well, the people forgot to be thankful, so venomous snakes appeared. They bit many people who died horrible deaths," added Mahlah.

"So much death, must we always talk about death? I am tired of the fighting, the plagues, and our mothers who give birth, only to see their children die," sighed Hoglah.

"But Yahweh sends mercy, too. Remember when Moses made a snake out of bronze and raised it high on a pole. Everyone who looked at that bronze snake and repented would live," Noah added a lighter note.

Bold Girls Speak

We took down our tent and loaded up our wagon, which we had to pull ourselves. Our poverty was evident compared to the other travelers. We did not have a donkey or oxen to pull our load, as many families did. With heavy hearts, we joined the procession that started creaking forward. We took one more glance back at the small mound where our father was buried, never to see him again.

"Hey, get moving. We are sorry your father died, but you can't hold up the caravan," the men behind us shouted. "We are moving toward Moab."

Every day we made progress toward the Jordan River. Sometimes we lugged the wagon uphill, other times we braced our backs against the front of the wagon to keep it from rolling downhill. Travel by itself was hard enough, but frequent fighting would also occur with the local inhabitants of whatever land we were passing through.

A cloud of dust rolled over the horizon toward us. It was the first frightful omen of an impending battle. Soon the ground would start to shake with the pounding of feet, a blast of trumpets, and then a crescendo of clanking weapons would follow.

"Why is Sihon, king of the Amorites, coming toward us with a huge army?" Tirzah asked. "Yahweh please, I don't want to see any more fighting."

"Sihon will not allow us to pass through his land, even though we promised not to use any water or take fruit from the fields," said Mahlah. She always knew these things.

"The lands of Ammon, Moab, and Edom are not promised to the Children of Israel, so they should know there is no danger that we will try to take them. The land of Canaan is our Promised Land. We would not be fighting them if they did not attack us first." Noah added. We had learned to trust that Yahweh would bring us victory, but it was hard to hold back the terror that gripped our dry throats.

The Israelite warriors rushed passed us to the front of the column with slings, bows, javelins, and swords. All of the rest of us fell back to relative safety, but we could certainly hear the cries and shouts of battle.

"How can we be sure that Yahweh really wants us to move on into this Promised Land? He constantly allows us to be attacked from all sides," Hoglah said. She always asked the hard questions.

"But Yahweh also always sees us through the hardships, doesn't he? The land may be promised to Israel, but the current residents refuse to acknowledge the rule of Yahweh. We have to strive toward possession with hardship and tears," Mahlah said, always putting things into perspective for us.

It was enough to trudge forward day after day, one weary step at a time. Suddenly foreign armies appeared, angry shouts and fighting broke out, and we watched helplessly from a distance until Yahweh turned the tide and the battle was won. Afterward, when the fighting stopped, we had to walk past the field strewn with enemy bodies, injured horses, and broken chariots. We gathered bits of iron from broken enemy swords, which was a precious find. The Israelites only had weapons of softer bronze, and we did not have chariots drawn by horses. The enemy had better weapons than we did, yet we won battles because Yahweh gave us protection.

"They could have let us pass through their land peacefully; the fighting didn't have to happen," Milcah observed.

"Why does Yahweh allow death to occur, even to enemies?" Tirzah asked. She was wise beyond her years.

"Why don't they join us in the worship of Yahweh, instead of their gods which are made by human hands? We have many foreigners with us that followed us out of Egypt," Noah said, offering a solution. "Besides, Yahweh promised that all nations would be blessed through Abraham. Many foreigners are included in our history."

We walked through empty villages where the women and children hid from us, only peering from behind vines and bushes like frightened animals. "I do not like the people being afraid of us," our littlest sister observed.

"Are the Amorites really so bad that we had to fight with them?" Hoglah asked. "They think their gods are true and do not know any better."

"They have heard about our God, Yahweh, and they can see how powerful, just, and, indeed, merciful he is, but their hearts are hard, they refuse to accept Yahweh," Mahlah observed. "They do frightful things in their worship of Baal that are too awful to mention, and our people are easily seduced into their practices," our wise oldest sister said. She knew more about these things. "Yahweh has demanded that these enemies be totally destroyed; how can we disobey Yahweh?"

All too soon, another battle followed. Og, the king of Bashan, blocked our path. We repeated often the song of Miriam: "Sing to the Lord, for he is highly exalted. The horse and its rider he has hurled into the sea." We tried to remember the wonders of Yahweh performed in the past. Again, Yahweh said to Moses, "Don't be afraid." However, how could we not be afraid? We never got used to the fighting.

DID THAT DONKEY TALK?

We were excited to be finally in sight of the Jordan River. Approaching Moab, a remarkable event occurred. Balak, the king of Moab was afraid of us. Even with all the hardships and battles, the population of the Israelites had increased. Balak was well aware of the battles that the Israelites had successfully fought. He said, "This horde is going to lick up everything around us, as an ox licks up the grass of the field."

"Balak, the king of Moab, is wise enough to not cause another battle, but did you hear the unbelievable action he is taking?" Hoglah asked.

"He has sent for Balaam, a seer from northern Mesopotamia. He practices divination and can call down curses and blessings," Mahlah said.

"He does what?" Tirzah looked puzzled.

"Apparently this man practices Babylonian astrological arts. Such people can call upon evil spirits to cause either blessings or curses upon a whole country. Balak is willing to pay a lot of money for this pagan seer to practice his powers of evil upon us." Mahlah had her ways of getting information.

"Can things get any stranger?" Milcah asked.

"Well, his idea seems to be better than fighting," observed Noah.

We gathered firewood some distance from the camp when we heard a shout of outrage. "Stupid beast, what are you doing? Get back on the road." A man was beating his donkey with a stick. It was a pathetic sight. We would have loved to rescue the animal, which, for a donkey, was unusually handsome. Light-colored animals, like this one, were reserved for high officials.

For the moment, we forgot our task and our eyes were diverted to the scene below. Peering through vines, we saw the man tug his donkey back to the path. He climbed astride again but did not progress very far. Between the stone walls bordering the fields, the path became very narrow.

"Donkey, you idiot ass!" the man yelled with pain when his foot was crushed against a wall. He pounded the poor animal again.

"Something supernatural is going on here. Donkeys just don't act like that," Milcah said. She knew animals. For the second time the man continued on his way. We followed behind, just out of sight. The path became so narrow that the donkey could barely squeeze through. Now suddenly, the animal's legs just buckled under the rider. Senselessly, the rider kept up the beating.

"What have I done to you to make you beat me these three times?" we heard braying across the valley. The voice was not human, yet we could understand it.

"Who said that?" we asked, stopped in our tracks.

"It is the donkey," said Milcah.

"Donkeys don't talk," said Noah. We all knew that of course.

"You have made a fool of me! If I had a sword in my hand, I would kill you right now." The rider answered back.

"Not only did the donkey talk, he thinks the donkey can hear!" Mahlah exclaimed. But she had no explanation.

"Am I not your own donkey, which you have always ridden, to this day? Have I been in the habit of doing this to you?" It was definitely the donkey talking.

"I am so glad that donkey is giving him a piece of her mind because he

Bold Girls Speak

hit her," Tirzah said in defense of the animal. Then she paused a moment, "Wait, that donkey just talked, but donkeys don't talk. That donkey talks, hears, and understands! I would like that donkey." Yahweh had once told Moses that the Israelites would see miracles never before seen among any other people. Our littlest sister has grown up with so many miracles in her short life, she thinks some events are normal that really are not.

"Why have you beaten your donkey these three times?" Yet another voice that sounded other-worldly, echoed from the sky. The drama was not over. "I have come here to oppose you, because your path is a reckless one before me. The donkey saw me and turned away from me these three times. If the donkey had not turned away, I would certainly have killed you by now."

"Whose voice was that?" we quietly exclaimed as the scene continued to unfold. Then we saw it. A fearsome angel was facing the donkey and rider, blocking the way.

"That man is Balaam the seer, the prophet that Balak sent for from the north!" Mahlah gasped while recovering from the shock.

The angel continued, "Go to Balak, but speak only what I tell you." This was quite enough for one day; we have seen an angel and a talking donkey.

"Do you think we should run back to camp and tell someone that Balaam is coming? They will want to know that he won't speak curses, but blessings on the Israelites," Hoglah said while keeping her head about her.

"Do you think they will believe us?" Milcah added.

"If they don't, they will have to endure the fear of curses until they hear blessings with their own ears," Noah observed.

Upon arriving back at the camp, we joined the multitude of the Children of Israel at the base of Mount Peor. Balaam the seer seemed to observe the flight of birds that soared above him, but he apparently did not perceive any patterns from that usual source of divination. Then Balak arrived on the scene. He and Balaam appeared to exchange angry words. Seven altars were already built for the sacrifice of seven bulls and seven rams. This was the third time that Balak had tried to get Balaam to pronounce a curse upon Israel. This was the third mountain, and the third preparation of seven alters. The difference on this third occasion was that Balaam could see all the Children of Israel watching, and they could see him. Balak's hope was that Balaam could see the multitude of Israelites spread out over the valley and finally understand the threat that Moab felt. Surely, Balaam would now curse the Israelites. Balak killed and offered a bull and a ram on each of the seven alters. The sisters knew that Yahweh never required seven sacrifices at once on seven altars.

The multitude held its breath with the expectation of hearing curses pronounced upon them. We already knew it was not to be as Balak had hoped. Balaam the seer could only let words of blessing come from his mouth. At the third trial, the Spirit of God came upon him and he uttered his oracle, "Their king will be greater than Agag; their kingdom will be exalted. God brought them out of Egypt; they have the strength of a wild ox. They devour hostile nations and break their bones in pieces: with their arrows they pierce them. Like a lion they crouch and lie down, like a lioness—who dare to rouse them? May those who bless you be blessed and those who curse you be cursed!"

Balak clapped his hands together in anger that Israel received blessings instead of curses, but there was nothing he could do. Balaam returned to his land without pay. We continued to gaze at the smoke that drifted upward from the seven sacrifices and the smell of burnt meat, hair, and bones. We had not eaten meat for a long time, and we were hungry just thinking about such a feast. We understood how an enemy, wealthy enough to afford to sacrifice so many animals, could be attractive. Yet these seven sacrifices by Balak were in vain, made to a false god, Baal. The real God of Israel is our strength and protection.

After the event was over, we walked to our tent as the sky became dark. We discussed the blessing that came out of the mouth of Balaam. "A star will come out of Jacob; a scepter will rise out of Israel," he had said. We discussed among ourselves, "What did that mean?"

THE SISTERS DARE TO ASK MOSES

"The priests are counting the entire population of Israelites for when they divide up between the tribes this Promised Land, which no one has seen," Milcah reported to us.

"What do they mean we will draw lots for land which we will actually own?" Hoglah asked. "I can't imagine actually owning anything and living in a house. I would just like to have sandals that hold together a little longer, although these are lasting remarkably well."

"Oh, they are taking a census all right, but only of the men. They are the only ones who will receive land," Mahlah, our worldly oldest sister said.

"We are only girls, what will happen to us?" young Tirzah asked, suddenly understanding the bigger issue. "And we will no longer have manna to eat? How can this be a Promised Land?"

"We will grow our own food. We will stay in one place long enough to plant grains and then harvest them," added in Noah. "The elders are already drawing maps with sticks in the dust. They write their names on stones and rearrange them endlessly like game pieces."

"But our names are not on the stones. Our father is dead, and as women we won't get land," Hoglah predicted.

"Well, we will certainly marry, then husbands will take care of us," our idealistic littlest sister piped in. She knew her stories about how our ancestor Jacob met Rebecca at the well, and how Moses also found his wife at a well.

"Hey, get realistic sister," said Hoglah. "Look at us. We are sunburned. Our skin is like leather, sand-blasted from the wind. No eligible young men will ever give us a second look, even if we are struggling with heavy jars to pull water up from the wells. We have to get land in order to eat."

"Besides, lately the Israelite men have preferred the Moabite women. Of course they haven't been walking every day for years, and can manage to wash their hair," Mahlah said to no one in particular. The rest of us did not pursue that topic, as Mahlah seemed bitter.

"Our father never regretted that we were all born female, at least he never expressed it," Noah sighed. "Yet he knew he would never live to see the Promised Land and receive his allotment of land. What would he want us to do?"

"It is a matter of justice," Milcah added. "Without a son, his family inheritance promised by Yahweh will disappear unless we advocate for ourselves."

Five Sisters Who Asked for Their Inheritance

"The area of land that our tribe, Manasseh, receives will be unfairly smaller," Hoglah observed.

"Father knew Moses and said he was a fair and good man. Maybe he would help us preserve our father's memory," Mahlah lightened up.

"Not to mention, provide us land to keep some sheep and grow crops for a living," Noah added.

"Do you know anything about planting a field?" Hoglah asked.

"Well then, we have two problems, no land, and we don't know wheat from a weed. All we have seen in this barren wilderness is manna and thorns that poke through our thin sandals," Milcah added.

"How does one eat wheat? I hear that it can be used to make bread, but I am not sure how wheat turns into bread," Tirzah said. She had little experience eating anything other than manna.

"So, which one of us is going to approach the great Moses and ask for an inheritance? I have heard that he actually talks to Yahweh, and once received the commandments from Yahweh on Mount Sinai," Noah was thinking aloud. We all fell silent at that thought.

"So, will Yahweh condemn us for daring to ask, and will he remember our loss?" Hoglah asked, unafraid of the hard question.

We all looked at each other. One of us would have to be very brave. But all of us together, we knew, could be braver still.

The Tent of the Tabernacle must be approached only with fear and reverence. Yahweh had given many laws concerning who had anything to do with it; people have been known to die if they came near inappropriately (Num 1:51). The tent that enclosed the tabernacle was made with precious fabrics and was surrounded by a fence made of linen curtains. From camp to camp, for almost forty years, the priests disassembled and rebuilt the whole complex at every new location. Hidden within the Holy of Holies was the Ark of the Covenant, a gold-plated chest that was carried by the Levites before the procession of the Israelites, whenever we moved. It represented the presence of God leading the way throughout all the travels. It was constructed many years ago, and it was made of the finest materials by skilled artisans according to the exact instructions given directly from Yahweh to Moses.

We hesitated at the gate when the curtain was pulled aside for us to enter. Compared to the dullness of our dusty, everyday lives, we seemed to be looking into the splendor of heaven. The morning incense had already been burned, leaving behind a fragrance that assaulted our noses with a heady sweetness.

"We are the daughters of Zelophehad," Mahlah told the guard at the gate of the enclosure. "May we approach Moses with a special request concerning our father's inheritance?"

"Come nearer, daughters of Zelophehad," we heard a voice from within call us. We hesitated to put one foot ahead of the other and progress into the enclosure. "I knew your father; I am sorry for your loss. Is there anything I can do?"

This was the first time that we had seen Moses up close. He wore the years of desert life in his deeply creased face. He and several other priests formed a line of gold-trimmed, heavily embroidered robes. Eleazar, Aaron's son, was the high priest. He was dressed in the ephod, or a sort of apron that was decorated with large gems of precious stones. Each stone represented one of the twelve tribes. We had never seen ruby, topaz, and sapphire stones, which reflected the morning sun with dazzling light. The whole effect of the tabernacle made us quite dizzy with its awesome majesty.

"Our father died in the desert, and he was a good man. He did not participate in the rebellion of Korah but died of old age," Mahlah said, daring to break the silence.

"He taught us well to serve Yahweh with fear and reverence. He told us all the stories of the Exodus and the forty days at Mount Sinai when you, Moses, received the law from the hand of Yahweh," added Noah.

"We are five sisters, without any brothers. Why should our father's name disappear from his clan because he had no son?" Hoglah continued.

"The tribe of Manasseh should not lose this land. We wish to receive our father's portion along with his male relatives in the Promised Land of Canaan," Milcah finished the request.

"Well, it is rather irregular that women would receive an inheritance of land. I will have to ask Yahweh about this unusual request," Moses thoughtfully replied.

"When do you next talk to Yahweh?" our littlest sister piped up. We had forgotten to tell her not to talk.

"Ahem," Moses had a rather shocked look on his tired old face. We were horrified that our whole cause could be lost. After an impossibly long pause, Moses spoke up again, "I can't really say; Yahweh speaks in Yahweh's own time, but I should get in one more talk before I see him face to face."

"What did he mean by that?" we gazed at each other. No one sees God face to face and lives to tell about it.

We retreated backwards a few steps before turning around. We were somewhat dejected. "Well what kind of answer did we get? Moses did not refuse us. We have to wait on Yahweh," Hoglah said, breaking the silence on the way to our tent.

"Were we too bold to ask for this exception?" we questioned among ourselves.

"You know women don't inherit land," some men taunted us. "There will be more land for us if you don't inherit. After all, do you know what to do with land?"

"Well none of us knows how to plant grains and vineyards. Our generation has never been settled in one place," Milcah reminded them.

"Will Moses die without giving us an answer?" we discussed that evening. It is amazing how the ancient evil one raised all kinds of doubts in our imaginings. The whole camp was aware that Moses would die before we moved over the Jordan. Moses would not set foot into the Promised Land, because of his disobedience at Kadesh many years earlier when he struck the rock for water instead of simply using speech (Num 20). Yahweh demands strict obedience and total trust, and his justice is fearful. Had we daughters of Zelophehad offended Yahweh by making an outrageous request?

Yahweh answers in Yahweh's own time, as Moses had said. In the evening, huddled around our campfire, we wondered. Was Yahweh as near as our breath or as far away as the stars? Can we approach Yahweh directly, or only the priests? Would Moses receive word before he died? Our request began to seem rather meager in contrast to much bigger questions; would we be lost in these cosmic events?

We heard that Moses was indeed getting words from Yahweh. He was receiving multitudes of words including commands about many kinds of sacrifices and numerous festival days, and laws about crossing the Jordan and entering the Promised Land. We learned that Joshua would be anointed Moses' successor. The scribes were busy with all the writing. Would the request of the daughters of Zelophehad be remembered in all the more important legislation?

Finally, though it was only a few days later, but seemed much longer, a messenger called us to the tabernacle. We were beyond mere fear; we were terrified until Moses opened his mouth. "My daughters, the word of Yahweh is thus: 'What Zelophehad's daughters are saying is right. You must certainly give them property as an inheritance among their father's relatives, and give their father's inheritance over to them.'"

Our weak knees barely carried us back to our tent. "Imagine, out of all the words of Yahweh that Moses has received and recorded, Yahweh has not forgotten us! Of all the grains of sand who are the children of Abraham, he has heard our request," we rejoiced together wildly. For the first time since the death of our father, we felt like we were just the width of the Jordan away from a new life in a new land.

Moses, at 120 years of age, died a short time after he delivered the message to us. We watched him ascend to the top of Mount Nebo with a spring in his step because he knew where he was going. But first Yahweh allowed him to look into the Promised Land. He never came back down. Yahweh buried him in a place that no one knows, and the Children of Israel wept for him thirty days. We, the daughters of Zelophehad, will always have this story to tell about how Moses heard our request. It was our privilege to have asked him personally. We will also learn how to plant grains, fruit trees, and vines, maybe even flowers.

Five Sisters Who Asked for Their Inheritance

POINTS TO PONDER ON THE DAUGHTERS WHO ASKED

The daughters of Zelophehad did eventually marry. Be sure to read Joshua 17:4 to find out how this story ends. Cities named Tirzah and Hoglah are still on the map of Israel today. The other daughters' geological areas were recorded several centuries later, but the locations have been lost since. These *Bold Girls* dared to approach Moses for a change in the laws that God had given earlier. As new situations occurred, adjustments in the law were occasionally made, and this is one example. The daughters received an additional requirement: they would have to marry men from the tribe of Manasseh so that their land would stay in that clan. One may think that the privilege of males to inherit was maintained in the end anyway, but note that the names of the daughters remained with the land many centuries later, not Zelophehad's nor the names of sons they may have had later. At the time they entered Canaan, Manasseh numbered fifty-two thousand people, so their choices of husbands was not limited! Land was actually owned by families and not individuals, and the Israelites acknowledged that ultimately all the land was God's. As this story illustrates, the great Yahweh, the Old Testament name for God, cares for women and girls, and grants their requests, not only for them, but for all the following generations.

Imagine that the only life you have ever known is wandering in a desert. The promised new land may hold a bright future for some, but for you the prospects are empty. You must survive alone with your sisters in a strange new land and, in addition, your parents are now dead. Your future is bleak if you do not find a man to marry you. Legitimate ways to earn a living are nonexistent for a woman, and you cannot inherit property. Try to find out as many details of the daily life in the wilderness travel from the biblical text as possible, and look up information in other reference books to better understand the routes the Children of Israel may have taken.

Why is this book of the Bible called Numbers? When the Israeli spies reported that the land of Canaan was inhabited by giants, the Children of Israel were afraid to go in and conquer this land. So, a census was taken at the beginning of their wanderings to count the *number* of fighting men.

God took very seriously this lack of trust in his power to overcome the enemy, and he sentenced the Children of Israel to wander for forty years. All people more than twenty years old died before the end of the wandering. This story is related in Numbers 13–14.

In the story of the five sisters, the constant complaining about having to eat the same food is described in the book of Numbers. Verses 11:7–9 explain how the manna appeared, how it tasted, and how the Children of Israel could prepare it in various ways. The Children of Israel often complained about conditions in the wilderness, and some even wished to return to slavery in Egypt. I tried to re-create the harsh wilderness conditions in this story. We wonder how they could have been so shortsighted as to wish they were back in Egypt, but try to think of yourself in the same situation. We are also quick to complain sometimes!

Not only were the conditions harsh with extremes of temperature, constant lack of water, and the same food every day. Constant fighting with nations that opposed them also occurred. This story brings up many questions about war, and the rightness of killing enemies. This is very hard to sort out. Is killing, even of noncombatants, ever mandated by God? In the wilderness journey and while conquering the Promised Land, it is clearly commanded by God to destroy the enemy, but this was at a time of very special circumstances in the history of Israel.

I find the story of Balaam and Balak to be one of the most bizarre in the whole Old Testament. Ancient Middle East kings engaged in the practice of using seers and diviners for advice in military decisions. Certain prophets had a reputation for special effectiveness and were much in demand for their services. Balaam was one of a profession of diviners or prophets who could be hired by kings to determine the future or call curses or blessings on command. Apparently, they must have been successful at least some of the time. Remember that Balaam was not an exclusive worshipper of Yahweh, yet Yahweh used him in this instance to convey a message to Balak, the enemy king of Moab, and give an encouraging blessing to the Children of Israel. If it was not strange enough that God used a foreign diviner to convey words of encouragement to the Children of Israel, God uses a lowly beast of burden, a donkey, to get Balaam's attention. Yet, the talking donkey is not the greatest miracle of the story. More fantastic was the working of the Spirit of God, who turned the words of cursing, which Balaam was being paid to pronounce, into words of blessing on the Children of Israel. By very dramatic means, Balaam was made aware that he was to speak only words of blessing and not curses onto God's people. The words that came out of his mouth were not the words he had planned to say. God will use what and whomever he will to accomplish his purposes.

Five Sisters Who Asked for Their Inheritance

QUESTIONS FOR DISCUSSION

1. Look up Joshua 16:3–6. Here is the continuation of the story of the daughters of Zelophehad. They do eventually get married and have families who continue to inhabit the lands for many generations. The villages of Hoglah and Tirzah can still be found today in Israel.

2. What is the history of the Children of Israel in Egypt? How did they get there and why are they now in the wilderness? Why did their parents die in the wilderness?

3. Why does this story follow the story of *Miriam Who Negotiated*? Review the story of Moses. Who was this man and how did he become the leader of the Children of Israel? Put these events on a timeline.

4. Read through the book of Numbers. How many different ways did the Children of Israel disobey God? What were the consequences of their disobedience? (Rejection of authority in Numbers 21:5, complaining Numbers 14:2.)

5. Look up Exodus 34:12–16 where God describes the separation that the Children of Israel should maintain with the other nations. What laws are included in these verses?

6. What was the Ark of the Covenant? What was its significance and why did the Israelites follow it? Look up drawings of how it may have appeared.

RELATED CULTURAL AND HISTORICAL QUESTIONS TO EXPLORE

1. Archaeological history is important to understanding the Bible. When was the Bronze Age and the Iron Age? As you read the *Bold Girls* stories, make a timeline to compare when each of these stories took place. The Israelites were behind their neighbors in acquiring knowledge of how to work with iron. How did that affect their way of fighting and conquering other cities?

2. Find a map of the possible routes that the Children of Israel took during the forty years of wandering. Where are the major stopping places mentioned in Numbers? (Mount Sinai at the beginning of the journey, Kadesh where Moses struck the rock for water, and the plains

Bold Girls Speak

of Moab, where this *Bold Girls* story took place). Into what kind of sin did the Children of Israel fall in each location?

3. Does the symbol of a snake wrapped around a pole remind you of a modern day symbol? It also is a foreshadowing of a symbol in the New Testament. What is it? What is the prophecy of Numbers 24:17: "A star will come out of Jacob"?

4. We may read with amusement that ancient people would believe in the power of pagan soothsayers and other forms of magic, but do we do the same thing today? What about in other parts of the world? Where else in the Bible is a person who practices this craft?

5. Can you imagine spending your whole childhood on a camping trip? Do some people constantly live in a similar situation now in the twenty-first century?

SUGGESTED TOPICS OF DISCUSSION FOR TEACHERS AND PARENTS OF OLDER STUDENTS

1. To the discussion of the various sins into which the Children of Israel fell during the wandering in the wilderness, add the falling into sexual immorality as described in Numbers 25:1–9. Why was it important for the Israelites not to be in contact with the Moabites? What were the evil practices in their worship of Baal?

2. Why did God demand destruction of the Canaanites? Leviticus 18 describes the sexual practices of the Egyptians and the Canaanites. Deuteronomy 23:17 condemns temple prostitution.

3. Discuss various objections raised against Christianity and religion in general by "the new atheists." In this discussion, include an exploration of God's demand for the complete destruction of "anything that moves" in holy war and a dedication of all the spoils of war to God.

4. What were the one-time qualifications applied in the Israelite holy wars of conquest when entering the Promised Land that are not valid for other wars? In Joshua 2:10 is the interesting story of an important woman named Rehab. She knew that God had demanded that Israel completely destroy their enemies. Is this fair, or is this command from God too cruel? What does this mean in warfare?

The Girl Who Spied

2 Samuel 14; 2 Samuel 17:17

A LESSON IN ACTING

"Help me, O King!" A woman with ragged clothes bowed deeply on the cold marble floor before David's throne. Her dirty face was engraved with streaks by the tears streaming down her cheeks.

"What is troubling you?" King David asked simply.

"I am indeed a widow; my husband is dead. I, your servant, had two sons. They got into a fight with each other in the field. Now all the relatives want to kill my remaining son. This is the only burning coal I have left, leaving my husband neither name nor descendant on the face of the earth."

"Go home, and I will issue an order on your behalf," answered the king. The woman seemed to hold her shoulders higher as she raised herself from the floor and started to turn toward the exit.

A servant girl had the assignment of opening and closing the court doors to allow access to King David. At her post, she heard all the entreaties of people who approached King David for favors. Most required heart-wrenching decisions, which David made with super-human wisdom. Only a few moments earlier, the two women, among the lowest ranked in the kingdom, exchanged uncomfortable glances when they met over the threshold. Then the servant girl stepped aside and out of sight behind a potted palm where she would wait until called to open the great doors again. Apparently, this case was over, so she stepped in front of the doors. But wait, the woman was not finished with her petition.

"Let your servant speak a word to my lord the king," she continued.

"Speak," David said with some surprise.

"So, do you not convict yourself, for you have not brought back your own banished son?"

The lowly widow dared to put the great King David on the spot! Every attendant in the room gasped. They all knew the truth about the king's son, Absalom, who three years ago had fled Jerusalem when he killed his half brother, another son of the king, Prince Amnon. Some people wanted Absalom executed as a murderer; others were not so sure. Now Absalom was the apparent successor to the throne after David. This supposedly poor widow had constructed her story parallel to the dilemma of David.

David answered the question with a question. "Has my army general, Joab, put you up to this?"

"Yes," she dared not lie. "It was your servant Joab who instructed me and put the words into my mouth. You, King David have wisdom like that of an angel of God. You know everything that happens in the land."

All ears in the throne room strained to hear every word. Lesser infractions of etiquette in the court had been known to cause heads to roll. What would David do to someone who tried to corner him? The woman, whose false identity as a grieving widow was now exposed, stood up proudly and walked out with a dignified bearing that betrayed her beggarly clothes. She knew she had influenced even the great King David to heal a family rift.

"Can you imagine? This encounter with the king was all acted!" The servants exclaimed later between themselves. "This woman is really known as the wise woman of Tekoa! She is not a poor widow at all. How easily we were all fooled, even King David, until he recognized the story as his own."

"What an actress!" The servant girl wondered to herself. She was amazed that the woman so effectively pretended to be someone she was not. "This skill of acting could come in very handy around the court," she continued. "But in reality," she thought to herself, "I do this every day. In this service, I am always pretending to be someone I am not. It is like wearing a mask. I pretend to know things I do not, I pretend not to know things I do know. It is a very tricky skill to survive in this palace world."

Joab, the great military leader, by employing the wise woman of Tekoa to carry out this deceit, succeeded in bringing the crown prince back to Jerusalem. However, the longed for reunion between King David and his son, Absalom, did not immediately take place face-to-face. Two great men, even though father and son, did not talk to each other; they both lived separately in their own residences. The return of Absalom drew great attention; he was so handsome he turned the heads of both men and women. The servants admired his magnificent hair, which was so thick that he had to cut it when it became too heavy. Locks of wavy hair were weighed and later appeared on the black market to be sold to adoring fans. A legend, started by those in a position to know, was that from the top of his head to the sole of his foot he had no blemish. He married and started a young family in Jerusalem, which included three sons and a daughter named Tamar, named in memory of his sister who was murdered by Amnon a few years earlier.

The men envied his natural ability to attract followers. When Absalom moved through the city, fifty young men would clear the streets to make room for his chariot, which was pulled by splendid horses. At the city gate, he made promises to people needing favors and claimed that if he were king, everything would be much better. Absalom stole the hearts of the people of Jerusalem by his good looks and slick promises. King David appeared to tolerate the audacious behavior of his son for four years, but never invited him to the palace.

DANGEROUS TIMES IN JERUSALEM

The servant girl did not understand why Absalom was allowed such free reign to disrespect his father. Acting as if he owned the place, the son brazenly anticipated the time when he would be king, since his father was getting along in years. David, unable to deny his son any wish, granted him his request to go to the city of Hebron to fulfill a vow and worship. Instead, Absalom had other intentions that were less pious; for in truth, he was conspiring to take over the throne. He sent messengers throughout the land with the message, "As soon as you hear the sound of the trumpets, shout 'Absalom is king in Hebron.'"

Messengers rushed to David and told him, "The hearts of the people of Israel are with Absalom." David was crushed with the hurt that his son, whom he loved, betrayed him.

"Come!" David told his officials that were with him, "We must flee, or none of us will escape from Absalom. We must leave immediately, or he will move quickly to overtake us and bring ruin upon us and put the city to the sword."

Absalom declared himself the legitimate ruler of Israel and announced his intention to take over the country. With the sound of the shofar he moved into the palace.

The servant girl remembered verses from the psalms, which were claimed to be written by David. They were repeated at times of sacred service and became a prayer in times like this. *It is time for You to act, O Lord, For they have regarded Your law as void* (Ps 119:126).

"What will this day bring?" The servant girl thought as she woke that morning. She was filled with a sense of foreboding. King David was leaving the city without a fight to avoid more bloodshed. He was horrified with the thought of fighting his own son in battle.

A rumor spread like wildfire through the palace. "They are removing the Ark of the Covenant from the Holy of the Holies." The servant girl did not know what to make of this news.

"For several years, no one has even seen the Ark of the Covenant except the priests on the Day of Atonement," other servants informed her. "It is housed in a tent on the highest mound of the city, on Mount Moriah, the ancient location where Abraham almost sacrificed his son, until an angel intervened."

Older servants added, "Some of us saw the ark when it was brought into Jerusalem. That was early in the reign of King David. It was a huge celebration, but with a dark side."

"A man died when he touched it," an elderly servant reminisced. "Yes, he only intended to stabilize it when it tipped from the ox cart. He innocently wanted to keep it from falling on the ground, and he was struck dead."

"Struck dead?" The servant girl could not believe it.

"Yes, the Ark of the Covenant has a long history. Moses built this same ark in the wilderness when the Children of Israel escaped from Egypt. In it are the most holy items of the people, the tablets on which God had written the Ten Commandments and a sample of manna."

"Oh, and David was seen frantically dancing, which upset his first wife, Micah," the elderly servant added. "She was banned from his presence forever after that incident. And to think, she was a daughter of Saul." Palace intrigue and gossip had kept tongues wagging for the many years of David's reign. It was impossible to believe there would no longer be a King David.

"We are going to go out to get just a peek of the ark as it is removed from the Tent of the Tabernacle," the servants were determined.

"But, I am not going to get too close," the servant girl thought, somewhat nervously. She recalled the words of Moses written on ancient scrolls. *They called upon the Lord, and He answered them. He spoke to them in the cloudy pillar; They kept His testimonies and the ordinance He gave them* (Ps 99:6–7).

The remaining household staff sadly watched the assembly move down into the valley, and then climb up the Mount of Olives.

"Who could have imagined? The great King David is weeping," the servant girls whispered to each other. The event was too solemn to speak about aloud. The most curious of the servants climbed the eastern wall of the city to observe the momentous event.

"He has covered his head and is walking barefoot down the trail followed by two priests, the Ark of the Covenant, and many soldiers," the servants said while straining their eyes to see the events.

"Why is he is pausing?" they asked.

Unexpectedly, when the procession reached the summit of the Mount of Olives opposite the valley from Jerusalem, David came to a halt and let everyone pass him.

"The priests have put down the Ark of the Covenant and are gathering stones to build an altar. We see flames and a wisp of smoke rising into the sky. David seems to be having a heated discussion with the priests," the servants reported to each other.

The servant girl, along with the other servants, guessed at the purpose of the discussion. Finally, David and the priests on the Mount of Olives seemed to come to an understanding.

"Carry the ark of God back to the city. If I shall find favor in the eyes of the Lord, he will bring me back, but if he say thus: 'I have no delight in thee,' behold, here I am, let him do to me as seems good unto him." Then the two high priests, Zadok and Abiathar, who were carrying the ark, reversed direction and returned to the city.

"Why is he not carrying the Ark of the Covenant for Jehovah's protection in battle?" The servants asked, dismayed. "Is he really entrusting it to Absalom?"

Two young sons of the priests, Jonathan and Ahimaaz, with David and his army, continued east until out of sight on the road toward the Jordan River.

Now neighbor was pitted against neighbor. Families and friends were divided over the issue. Who was the real king? Father or son? No one knew for sure.

The servant girl was bewildered and feared for her future. No one thought to tell the servants where they should go or what they should do.

When the priests came back, she quickly made herself useful as a servant with one of them, Zadok. The girl was not certain if her new master was supporting Absalom or David. She could not imagine that he would change allegiance. Everything was very hush-hush in the large household of the priest. She really needed her acting skills, which were improving, and she observed everything.

Gossip was running wild, and abominable deeds were committed during the takeover. Eyes were averted from the atrocities committed on the rooftop of the palace. No one knew who was for Absalom and who was still loyal to David. Not that she paid much attention to rumors, for the steady stream of intrigue and gossip from the palace was rising to a shrill pitch.

Before all the recent events, for the first time, peace had seemed possible. David had united the twelve tribes of Israel, stretching from north to south, after years of war. Enemies were banished and the surrounding countryside subdued. It was the time to reap the benefits of all the building and conquest. Instead, it had come to this.

Pray for the peace of Jerusalem; May they prosper who love you. Peace be within your walls, Prosperity within your palaces (Ps 122:6).

A MISSION FOR A GIRL

Unexpectedly, one morning the servant girl was called to her master. This was always occasion for apprehension. Had she done something wrong? Only a few days had passed since she started working for the high priest. He did not yet know her tendency to dawdle in the market too long, and she certainly did not have vacation time coming to visit her family in the country. Surely she could not have already done something questionable to get her in trouble.

"Come into my chamber as soon as your duties and errands are finished," her master's message had instructed. She swept, polished, dusted, and tried to remember all her duties, but Zadok's beckoning was a major distraction. Finally, close to noon, she approached the servant who guarded his door.

"She is all right, let her in," she heard her master call from inside. The room was heaped with tablets and scrolls. Zadok dismissed the scribes who were working with him and glanced around to be sure the walls had no ears.

The Girl Who Spied

"What do you think of King David?" he asked her in a low voice. "How do you like it that his son, Absalom, has taken over his palace and even his concubines?"

These were dangerous questions. She gulped and took a deep breath. Should she act opposite of how she really believed? She knew the story of how David became king long ago. When he was young, he had killed the giant, Goliath, with a sling. He had great faith in the Jehovah God, whom he said helped him win on that day. She was not quite sure where her master's loyalty lay. She would have to take a chance and decided to be herself instead of acting.

"I think King David is a great king and what his son did was wrong. He should have waited to become king until his father was ready to appoint him." She paused and tried to read her master's face for approval or disapproval. He nodded to indicate interest in her continuing opinion. "Now there is more war and senseless killing. Absalom would become king anyway. He just had to wait longer. All the building and improvements that David has started in Jerusalem will come to an end."

Zadok's face registered interest and approval. The girl's heart was pounding. What was this all about? She told herself, "Act calm, control your voice."

"I need someone like you to carry out an important mission. This someone must be brave and must remember instructions exactly. I think you are the best person in the household to carry out this task," he said.

"How could this be me since I am the youngest and lowest ranked of anyone who lives here?" The girl kept this thought to herself, but her master must have read the quizzical expression on her face. She was not doing a good job of disguising her real thoughts.

"You are the best person because you are the one who would be the least noticed. A servant girl is not likely to arouse suspicion. You are also a quick thinker, and I notice how you can talk your way out of a tight spot," he continued. A tight spot? She did not like the sound of that! "Would you carry out a brave mission to help King David?"

"What could I possibly do to help the king?" she mumbled under her breath.

"Sure," she said aloud with a confident voice. She was not feeling so brave on the inside, but she was proud that he thought she was acting brave. "What should I do?"

Bold Girls Speak

"Well, you know my son, Ahimaaz, and the son of the other priest, Jonathan. It will be important that you can recognize them, even if they are well disguised," Zadok further explained.

"Oh, you mean they will be acting like someone they are not?" Now she realized how much she had just disclosed her stupidity. But Zadok did not notice.

"Very likely, but to complicate matters, Absalom has spies all over to watch out for people like you who are carrying messages. They are also pretending to be someone else."

The servant girl was getting somewhat confused. "I should not appear to be who I am," she thought, "and the spies who may be looking for me will not look like spies. Meanwhile the young men who I need to meet are also in disguise. Okay, this is clear," the girl gulped and reassured herself.

Only a few minutes later, she paused outside the massive East Gate of Jerusalem to survey the serpentine path that stretched far below her. Shading her eyes from the harsh sunlight, she pulled a scarf over her head. Hopefully, it would also keep anyone from recognizing her face. Then she took the first step to descend into the Kidron Valley. She casually hung a coarse woven bag over her left shoulder. Thankfully, she had no time to get nervous over the mission she was about to undertake. She played the part perfectly and looked like any other servant girl going into the valley to fetch produce for her household. In the city, she would not attract attention. Servant girls like her were practically invisible as they scurried through the streets on their many errands. Outside the city walls, the world was different. In the last weeks, so much had changed. Familiar words came to comfort her. *Yea, though I walk through the valley of death, I will fear no evil* (Ps 23:4).

The Girl Who Spied

She set off on the steeply descending trail to En-Rogel, which was a spring located south of the city walls. In her bag was a message to give to two young men. One of them, Ahimaaz, her master's son, was a friend of hers. He could run like the wind. According to plan, after she handed the leather scroll to him, he would indeed need to run to get it to David's troops in time. She hoped he was not already waiting at the spring. The other priest's son, Jonathan, she also knew because she had often seen both boys together in her service to David. This was a precarious and dangerous assignment. And if she was found out? She did not want to consider that. *Cause me to know the way in which I should walk, For I lift up my soul to You* (Ps 143:8).

She took a deep breath and gingerly tested the stability of the loose gravel. Alone with her thoughts, she reviewed recent events. The city of David had been a building site for more than the total thirteen years of her life. A new palace, housing the king with his many wives and children, towered over the east wall, commanding a magnificent view of the city entrance. King David sent for many precious materials to build it, including cedar from Lebanon. The old walls and terraces of the Jebusites, from whom the high, narrow strip of land had been conquered, were newly replaced or fortified. King David had made marvelous improvements to the city, making it a worthy capital of the nation of Israel. *Great is the Lord, and greatly to be praised, in the city of our God, His holy mountain. Beautiful in elevation, the joy of the whole earth, is Mount Zion in the far north, the city of the great King* (Ps 48:1–2).

"Ouch!" someone should tend to this path," she shouted aloud. Her foot shot out from under her and she fell, loosening a number of pebbles that rolled noisily down the slope. She abruptly jerked her mind from the events of just a few days ago. "I must concentrate on the present and keep my mouth shut," she thought. "Too often my thoughts become so real I start speaking them aloud. If this message falls into the wrong hands, I would be responsible for letting the true loyalty of my employer and other brave spies be discovered. I would be in big trouble, not to mention the lives of the whole household would be threatened. The sooner I arrive at En-Rogel, the quicker the whole mission to save David and the army will be underway. With every moment lost, the likelihood of success decreases. I am not hurt. I better get up and step even faster! Hold it! If I obviously rush, I will attract attention; people will stare and question. Slow down!"

Now, there was no way that the priests' sons would know she was the person meeting them at En-Rogel. Their only instructions were to look for someone from the household who would hand them the message. That was a problem. If they came closer to the city, the wrong person may recognize them, and they could be seized by Absalom's supporters. Venturing this close was dangerous enough. She had to arrive at the spring first, so they would not have to hang around. On the other hand, she could not act as if she was waiting around to meet someone, or she would attract unwelcome attention. This mission was all very tricky.

She rehearsed the various possible excuses to explain her presence at En-Rogel. Carrying the bag could give the appearance of doing many different things like picking berries, getting grain, or gathering firewood. However, the truth be told, if someone seriously started to pry, she would have a hard time explaining the reason for a maid of the high priest being in this area. Actually, the high priest had everything provided for in his household, because he received a portion of the sacrifices that were made at the temple for his upkeep. He did not have to support himself and his household in any other way. Of course, if someone insisted on looking into her bag, they would find the parchment, which was sealed with wax and the chief priest's imprint, then the mission was all over for her. Actually, not too many people could read the squiggles on the rolled up leather. She wished that she could. The sons of the priests would be able to read the message because they went to school. If someone did ask her what it said, she would not have to pretend ignorance; she really did not know what the words said.

She passed the Gihon Spring, and glanced to see who was hanging around. Wherever water was drawn, a gathering place formed, attracting not only friends and neighbors but also people with unknown purposes. This fountain was the main source of water for the whole city, and so it was a very busy place. Today she did not pause here, but hurried by. Another spring was her destination. En-Rogel was also an important meeting place, and it was very urgent that someone was waiting for her when she arrived. If everything went well.

She safely descended the steep slope leading away from the city and progressed on the path heading west. She walked in the shade of olive groves and past grape vines. Now the sun shone directly overhead. On her left was the graveyard. The dead were considered to be unclean and had to be buried outside the city walls. Sadly, she thought of the many new graves recently dug, and she rushed to get past this area. The king's lovely gardens lay at the base of the steep slope at the foot of the city of David, fed by runoff from the Gihon Spring. As tempting as it was to linger and enjoy the fragrances, she had to resist and press on.

The path was well traveled by both men and women, mostly workers. She kept her eyes down and tried not to attract attention. She pretended that she only had a small snack in her bag and did not clutch it too close. "Sun, slow down; I hope I am not taking too much time," she prayed. She thought about the two young men who were also approaching En-Rogel at the same time from the Jordan valley. Were they safe? What would she do if she did not find them? That thought caused a knot to form in her stomach. She had to keep walking in the hot sun to find out. *Be gracious to me, O God, be gracious to me, For my soul takes refuge in Thee; And in the shadow of Thy wings I will take refuge, Until destruction passes by* (Ps 57:1).

MAKING A DANGEROUS CONNECTION

A man was approaching her. He stared at her bag. She fought the urge to grip it closer. Instinctively she slipped her hand inside. The first thing she felt was a crust of bread. She pulled it out and started to chew on it.

"That is fine wheat bread you have young lady. What is your business in the middle of the day?" he asked. She then realized that poorer people outside of the city would most likely eat bread made from barley.

"I am fetching wheat from my master's field," was her practiced reply.

"You are a maid from a fine household, who is your master?" he asked.

"I work for a high priest," she could not lie, but she would not say more than she had to. She wished she had remembered to wear clothes that were more tattered, because outside the city walls even her maidservant's clothes would stand out.

"Ah! They are followers of David. They were seen leaving the city behind him," he pointed out.

"The priests are back in the city now," she informed him.

"Then are they supporting Absalom?" he asked, seeming to be surprised.

"It appears so. Do you want some bread?" she asked, quickly changing the subject.

The man greedily took some and murmured thanks. Then he seemed to lose interest in her and he went on his way. *The Lord is on my side; I will not fear. What can man do to me?* (Ps 118:6).

"Praise be to Jehovah!" she whispered to herself. She suddenly had a new realization of the possible danger she could meet. How much further? She continued to follow the path of the Kidron Valley past small fields of grain. Soon she came to the junction where this valley joined with the Hinnom Valley. *I sought the Lord, and He answered me, And delivered me from all my fears* (Ps 34:4).

A huge upright stone was coming into view that vaguely resembled the shape of a dragon. "That must be it!" she thought. En-Rogel was said to be the site of ancient religious rites and sacrifices. As she expected, several people were resting around the pool, drinking and napping in the shade. Others were just waiting, looking for something known only to them. That was the scary part: who could be spying on whom? She scanned the figures from afar, hoping to see someone familiar. As she got closer, it appeared that no one took notice of her, but this was tricky. It seemed that everyone, casually sitting on various rocks, was making an effort to blend into the landscape. Yet, they were all discretely observing each other very keenly. Anyone could be spying on her. She was relieved that Ahimaaz and Jonathan had not yet arrived, but she was worried that she would be exposed to whomever may decide to question or harass her. *Though I walk in the midst of trouble, You will revive me; You will stretch out Your hand Against the wrath of my enemies, And Your right hand will save me* (Ps 138:7).

She put on casual airs and tried to act older than she was. By now, she was dusty and sweaty, so she did not appear to be a maid from a fine house anymore. Her hair fell disheveled around her dirty face, and she was glad to rest on a shady rock. Momentarily closing her eyes, she sighed a prayer that the young men would arrive safely. She heard whistling from the distance, but paid no further attention. A few minutes later, she heard it again, but upon looking, only saw a couple of elderly shepherds approaching. Wait, something about their way of walking did not seem so elderly. They were looking directly at her. She became suspicious and got up to move away, but then she recognized the tune that one was whistling. She had heard it often in the court of David. Oh yes, it could be!

They abruptly turned away from the spring and returned in the direction from which they came. The girl waited a few minutes and then casually got on her feet as though she had to continue her journey. Moving away now, the "old shepherds" seemed to be dawdling; she hoped she was right about her instincts. Around the bend and out of sight of the spring, the shepherds paused. They were waiting for her to catch up with them. She still could not be sure, they had unkempt stubbly faces. But when she got closer, they also had big grins for her. It was hard not to give Ahimaaz a big hug, since they were old friends and he was just a few years older than she was, but she had to act like they were strangers.

She quickly passed him the parchment with the message. That was their only contact. No more could be risked. They continued to walk parallel a few steps, and then she slowed her pace and pretended to inspect some grape vines. If anyone had observed, they would have only seen their sleeves brush together briefly. Just before the boys were out of sight, she turned to watch them climbing the hill. She wanted to shout to them, "Slow down, you are giving away your disguise!" But then someone would certainly hear. She whispered a prayer that they would stay out of trouble. Then she hurried back to the city with a much lighter load, although the return trip was a steep climb.

Praise the Lord! Praise, O servants of the Lord, Praise the Name of the Lord! Blessed be the name of the Lord From this time forth and forevermore! (Ps 113:2).

POINTS TO PONDER ABOUT A GIRL WHO SPIES

Now Jonathan and Ahimaaz stayed at En-Rogel, for they dared not be seen coming into the city: so a female servant would come and tell them, and they would go and tell King David (2 Sam 17:17).

This whole *Bold Girls* scenario is based on just a few words. We do not know anything about this servant girl, but we do know quite a lot about the events in David's Jerusalem at this time. The places still can be found; the geography of the land and the basic layout of the city have not changed. Therefore, putting it all together, a story similar to this could have happened. Certainly, we know that a servant girl carried out an important part of the mission of transporting vital information between David's spies in Jerusalem and his army encamped near the Jordan River. Here is a case where the "best man" for the job was a girl. This was a job that a girl was uniquely qualified to carry out because she was most likely to be overlooked as someone who may be a threat. Yet, she had to be skilled enough to carry out the plan discretely, not to mention physically fit enough to walk down and back up a steep slope! Jerusalem is still today a city on a hill surrounded by deep gorges.

For some reason, these few words of information have been included in the story of David. This servant girl should not be overlooked. For young people it is a little treasure. There is indication she may have carried messages more than once. From these few words, we can be sure that the mission carried some danger, perhaps a great deal of danger, and we know that the assignment was important. From the Bible reference, we do not know if she used her voice, but we can safely assume that she had to be prepared to speak and apply some good sense and wisdom. We do not know in whose house she could have worked, and this part of the *Bold Girls* story is totally imaginary. She could have easily worked in the house of one of the two high priests at that time. Just think of what she had witnessed and learned by living in such an environment. If only we could know more about her!

This reference to a girl is the first example of a pattern we will discover in Bible stories. Many of the *Bold Girls* featured in this series are unnamed servant girls. Frequently in the Bible, the nameless, most lowly members of society have done very important work. Perhaps when she arrived safely back in the house of Zadok, he thanked her, but perhaps not. We know that God knows her by name, and her trust in him for safety and wisdom is counted to her for righteousness. Unknown numbers of young servants have done their jobs to the best of their ability, and this was also their only reward.

Why are the Psalms quoted throughout this story? Most of the Psalms were written or compiled by David. They were part of the common language of the priests and worship at this time, and so phrases that later appeared in a particular Psalm may have been already well known to the worshippers of Jehovah, including this girl. The Psalms have been a source of comfort and strength to God's people from the time of David to the present. They were also reassuring to the girl in this story. Have you read the Psalms and thought about the times in which they were written? If you are not familiar with either the Psalms or biblical events, then this story serves as a good introduction to both. Are you fascinated with the life of David, starting with his confrontation with Goliath? If so, you are not alone. This is usually one of the most memorable stories of the Old Testament for young people.

The wise woman of Tekoa at the opening of the story is from 2 Samuel 14. Be sure to read the Bible text and note the conversation that I included in this story, and the text I omitted. The story from the Old Testament is told with much detail. It was an imaginative manipulation that Joab designed to get David to ask his son back into Jerusalem. Unfortunately, the plan eventually backfired with many unintended results. When Absalom returned to Jerusalem, he led an uprising against his father, King David. Absalom was killed when his hair got caught up in a tree as he rode a horse in battle (2 Sam 18:9).

I tried to add context for the scene by showing it through the eyes of this most remarkable servant girl. It is always interesting to imagine these momentous events from the viewpoint of the lowly people. Observing the court of David through the eyes of a young person in the lower levels of society, as many of the *Bold Girls* stories do, adds new information to old stories, and makes the story more interesting to young people.

QUESTIONS FOR DISCUSSION

1. What happened to the sons of the high priests after they left En-Rogel? (See 11 Sam 18:18–21.) They had a narrow escape, and a woman helped them in a very original manner. Look up these verses and see how the story continues.

2. Here is a list of other women who helped David at different times. Who are these women and what did they do?

Wise woman of Tekoa (2 Sam 14:1–20)

Wise woman of Abel-Beth-Maacah (2 Sam 20:14–22)

Abigail (1 Sam 25; 1 Sam 27:3)

Michal (1 Sam 19:11–17)

Abishag (1 Kgs 1:1–4)

3. David had many wives. Why don't we form families in this way today? How many children did David have? Who finally did follow him as king? (See 1 Kgs 2:1–4.)

4. Why is the Ark of the Covenant important in this story and where else does it occur in the Bible? What was worship like at this time? How was it different than today? What do we know about the Ark of the Covenant?

5. How was music important to David?

6. How does this story continue for Absalom? What happened to King David?

Bold Girls Speak

RELATED CULTURAL AND HISTORICAL QUESTIONS TO EXPLORE

1. This story took place about the year 1000 bc What else was going on in the world at that time? What inventions were new?

2. Absalom was very good looking and attracted a popular following by making many promises. Is physical attractiveness a quality necessary for good leadership? Can you think of people like Absalom who attract large followings because they are handsome? Are attractive people happier?

3. Do you think this story is realistic the way it was written? How would you change it, or what other adventures could you imagine happening to a girl carrying out such a mission at this time?

4. How did young people live at this time, both boys and girls? Wealthy and poor?

SUGGESTED TOPICS OF DISCUSSION FOR TEACHERS AND PARENTS OF OLDER STUDENTS

1. In 2 Sam 16:21–22 the concubines of David are mentioned. What was the status of concubines compared with wives? Why were David's concubines abandoned in the palace after he left? What happened to them (2 Sam 20:3)? Note: high status men often took concubines who were women of lower status, such as former slaves, and who would not be considered suitable women to be wives.

2. Polygamy was practiced by several of the patriarchs and Israelite kings. Lamech, Gen 4:19; Abraham, Gen 15:2; Jacob, 29:21–30; David, 2 Sam 3:2–5; Solomon, 1 Kings 11:4–5. How did this eventually work out for them?

3. Why did Absalom kill his half brother, Amnon? What was David's reaction to this crime committed against his daughter by her half brother?

4. How successful was David as a father? Would you consider him a model of good parenting?

The Servant Girl Who Boldly Witnessed

2 Kings 5

TERROR IN THE NIGHT

A Hebrew girl raced frantically into the night. Thorny shrubs slashed her legs and arms, but did not slow her escape. Moments earlier, she had been fitfully dreaming, surrounded by her family, asleep in their mud brick home of Gilead.

"God, wake me from this nightmare!" she shrieked, and dug her fingernails into her clenched fist, trying to wake from the terror. The sharp stones that jabbed her bare feet were not just a bad dream. Where was a cave or even a large rock? Where she could hide and catch her breath? Will no one rescue her? People were fleeing in every direction. Her eyes pierced the dancing shadows thrown by flames that leaped from the roofs of her village behind her. Flashing swords blocked yet another path as she dashed back and forth to find safety. Branches crashed around her and horrible screams filled the crisp night air. Relief was nowhere. Her lungs were burning and her body trembled like that of a trapped creature.

Syrian soldiers were rumored to be in the area. Little wonder that now it came to this! Curse those self-important men in high places who decide a piece of land was worth fighting for, that some vain point of honor must be defended, or revenge must be extracted! Who pays the price for such arrogance and stupidity? We, the small ones who have no voice, who are never consulted, but are left for dead, bloody, crying, and violated. God, where are you? What right does another human have to decide that my life, small as it is, will end this terrible night? Does it matter I have dreams, people I love, who love me? . . .

The sound of horse hooves was closing in fast behind her. Her knees turned to clay. A blunt object swiftly cracked the back of her skull. As she slumped into the hard gravel, the last thing she saw were the crisp pinpoints of a million stars in the midnight sky. Her mind went blank and she knew nothing anymore.

A brilliant sun pierced her eyelids as she regained consciousness. Could it be the next day? Where was she? She shivered. A sharp pain stabbed her head with every movement. She struggled to put two thoughts together, but could not recall what had hit her in the head. She remembered a galloping horse. Hard hoofbeats. She found herself lying on a pile of packed straw. Someone had laid her there, and it smelled as though goats had recently been at home in it. She looked up. Other children from her village were protectively huddled around her limp body. Her heart leaped when, through a daze, she began to recognize her friends.

She mustered a few words through her lips. "Are we still in Israel?"

The boys and girls who were not crying whispered among themselves. "What are they going to do to us?" A girl told her, "Someone scooped you up and put you in the back of a wagon when they noticed you still had life in you. We have traveled all night on horses and in chariots. The soldiers attacked our village, and we are being carried off to Syria. They put us in an animal pen for the night. Maybe we are already in the territory of the enemy and on our way to Damascus."

"What happened to our mothers and fathers?" other children asked.

All of their stomachs churned from fear and hunger.

Soldiers stood a short distance away around a crackling fire. Their shiny shields and swords had been thrown in a heap nearby. It seemed so cruel that they were enjoying themselves with laughter and storytelling.

"Oh, to be closer to that fire and feel some warmth!" the girl said. "Do they think we are animals with fur coats and don't feel the cold?" Soon the smell of grilled lamb drifted across to them.

"Maybe we will get something to eat?" The children's teeth chattered, but nothing was offered. Finally, some soldiers staggered empty-handed toward the pen. The children held their breaths. "Was this going to be good or bad?"

"I could use help with my livestock," a gruff voice noted.

"I need some strong lads to herd sheep," a man was heard saying.

The Servant Girl Who Boldly Witnessed

"I would sure like to bring my wife a nice maid, a smart girl that can wait on her and be a companion when I am away," another deep voice added.

The children instinctively backed away from the men as they approached, clearing a path for the soldiers to walk through their huddled group. They rubbed their chilled arms. The sobbing subsided in anticipation of what fate awaited them.

"I don't like being looked at the way these men are staring at me." The girl squirmed. She kept her eyes down trying not to attract any attention to herself.

"I'll take this maid." A strong hand took her by the shoulder and led her away. She dared one last glance back at the rest of the children. When would she see familiar faces again?

"Come with me," she guessed the man to say. The voice was not as cruel as she would expect from an enemy. If only she could ask him questions, but she did not really understand his way of speaking.

They approached a scattered campsite of horses, chariots, and other soldiers. She interpreted the nod of his head and gesture to mean for her to climb into the bed of a two-wheeled wagon. Equipment was hurriedly loaded, and the small company started creaking forward. She had never ridden in a wagon with wheels before. In other circumstances, what an adventure this would have been! Now, she just shivered from fright and exhaustion. As they rolled away, she fought to stay awake, but the rocking motion caused her eyes to droop. She collapsed into a heap with her head resting against a soft bag of grain. The warmth of the sun's rays finally penetrated the dark robe that someone had thrown over her, and she fell asleep.

FAR FROM ISRAEL, AND LONELY

As the sun moved across the sky from east to west, the caravan made only brief stops to rest the horses. "Here, have some dates." The man indicated she should help herself from a bag. His voice was somewhat kind. "Try drinking some of this; you need the fluid." This dark drink tasted fizzy and strange to her. She fell asleep again.

She woke up later in the afternoon. When her head stopped throbbing, she almost enjoyed peering out of the chariot to watch the countryside pass by. They were moving so fast! The wind rushed past her ears and villages passed by in a blur. They had joined a major road, which she took to be the well-known King's Highway. Numerous wagons and caravans passed by, some carrying exotic looking people and merchandise. Everyone was in a hurry, traveling both directions, by foot, on camelback, and on horses. What a parade! Now she knew they were on the way to Damascus. What would await her there?

She was riding in a wagon driven by the high-ranked officer who had chosen her that morning. It was loaded with what little booty the soldiers had ransacked from her poor village. Besides the bags of grain and jars of olive oil on which she was sitting, the Syrians had not found much. It was late fall, and without this food her village would now hardly survive the winter. The thought brought tears to her eyes. She curled up again in the robe and decided this was her new home. There were no other females in her traveling party. The men of this group thankfully left her alone. She noticed that the man in whose chariot she was riding intimidated the other clean-shaven soldiers who eyed her.

The countryside gradually flattened out into a landscape of pastures. A large mountain loomed over the western horizon as they traveled north. Could that be the famous Mount Hermon? Finally, fertile fields and orchards of an oasis became visible in the distance after they crossed a large river. So much water, all at once, was frightening to the girl. Water swirled around the chariot wheels, but the horses seemed to like it.

It was long after dark when they arrived at the massive gates of a large walled city. Was this Damascus?

"Who goes there, and what is your business?" Animated conversation took place between the gatekeepers, and it seemed they would not get permission to enter. Gruff voices grumbled, "Wait until morning, the gate is shut!"

"Please, oh, please, I want to get out of this wagon," the girl prayed under her breath. She was stiff, cold, and very hungry. The girl sensed that life would improve for her in the city and she was anxious to get inside walls.

Finally, she dared a peek over the edge of the wagon. Unfortunately, a guard caught her movement, and she froze with fright in the glare of a flaming torch.

"Oh it is you, General Naaman, of course, I see you have a child with you. We will open up the night gate." He saluted respectfully as they rolled by. Well, she did not think she was a child, but it certainly turned into an advantage.

The Servant Girl Who Boldly Witnessed

The wagons and horses disturbed the nighttime silence as they clattered down a straight thoroughfare. Various members of the traveling party disappeared down narrow side passages to find their own places. Finally, their wagon rolled away from the others, and they entered into the walled compound of what must have been the palace of an important family. When they creaked to a stop, she stiffly climbed out of the wagon onto the cobblestone surface of a courtyard.

"Good evening, Master Naaman," a kind-voiced servant woman greeted them. "I see that you have rescued a strong, young maid." *Rescued? I was stolen*, thought the girl with indignation.

"Come with me, young one." She was led into a large house where another woman with friendly eyes gave her bread and warm broth. How good that felt! Her heart began to lift with the faint hope of a future.

"Here is some water for a wash, which you sure could use. I can tell you have been living with soldiers." Then the girl was shown a simple mat in a corner by the fire for sleeping. As she drifted off, she suddenly remembered it had been what seemed like an eternity since she last prayed.

"Forgive me, God, for not praying," she whispered. "It has been a little hectic lately . . . right, you know that already. Oh dear Jehovah, I pray that my family has survived. Keep them well, wherever they are. Will I see them again? Oh, and I thank you that my head does not hurt anymore. Praise be to you, Jehovah." Soon she was dreaming of old times in the land of Israel.

STRANGE SACRIFICE IN A STRANGE LAND

Months passed and finally she did not cry herself to sleep anymore. She longed for her simple home in Gilead and constantly worried about her family, but her life was physically comfortable, even if her heart sometimes ached.

She had a completely new life as the personal maid of the wife of the Syrian army general, Naaman. She slept on a comfortable cot outside of the door of her mistress's room. Her work was not hard. Sometimes a call would awaken her in the middle of the night to carry out a chamber pot. That really was the only unpleasant errand.

Her mistress actually slept on a piece of furniture called a bed, with wonderfully soft cotton linens from Egypt. She was enchanted with the fragrant collection of combs, ointments, and perfumes in bottles of ivory and alabaster that her mistress owned.

"Come here, you must learn how to mix this color." The mistress of the house put a beautiful, breakable flask in her hand. "Now trace a line around my eyes, see how it makes them look bigger." She opened another beautiful jar that was closed with a tight plug. "Wow, what a fragrance! It smells like a million flowers," the girl exclaimed as she poured a few precious drops into the warm bathwater of her mistress. She had only heard about such items from the prophet Elisha. He told stories about the evil queen Jezebel in Samaria who lined her eyes with green. The girl had been somewhat hesitant to use the colorful palette because of that story. However, she also remembered that women among her ancient grandmothers, like Sarah and Rebecca, were known for their beauty. Maybe they had used such secret ingredients as well. One day she dared to pick up a polished bronze plate and looked at it more closely.

"Who is the girl looking back at me?" The foggy image startled her, and she polished the mirror again. "I do not look like a Hebrew girl anymore at all! When did I turn into a Syrian servant girl?" Only her own voice echoed back. She had rarely seen her reflection on the surface of water puddles after the few rains that came in the winters of Gilead. "I even look older!" She was a little bit proud of that!

"I don't know who I am anymore," she said to herself in an imaginary message to her family. For the first time she had seen fragments of clay with mysterious markings etched upon them. The markings rather looked like a bird had walked across the wet clay and left tracks. How could these scratches speak to Master Naaman? He could get words from far away by looking at them. She desperately wished someone would carry such a tablet to her home in Gilead with such a message. Yesterday had been a terrible day. The strangeness of Damascus was often overwhelming and she was so homesick. If only she could ask her mother and father, anyone, for advice. But she was alone, surrounded by foreign customs and frightful images that crowded her thoughts.

It was a festival day. The whole household had been looking forward to it. The preparations were strange to her, and she could not truly imagine what would occur at the festival, but she knew it would be exciting. All the servants had extra jobs to get ready for it.

The Servant Girl Who Boldly Witnessed

"Look at the handiwork of the Hebrew servant girl," the older servants exclaimed with awe. "She has very nimble fingers." She enjoyed practicing this new craft of fabric making and never dreamed that such beautiful things could be made. Damascus was known for the manufacture of rugs and tapestries. The latest fabric was the most beautiful she had ever made, but who was going to wear it in a garment? However, she sighed, such luxury she would gladly give up in a minute to be back home in her village in Gilead.

"Help me dress," her mistress commanded that morning. "Today is the great feast day of Rimmon Hadad. You will see the marvelous procession, but stay close to my side, and pick up my robe if the street is dirty." The servant girl was disappointed her lady was not wearing the robe that she had just finished. Every member of the household, even the servants, received new clothes, but none were as fine as the garment she had sewed. Once they left their quiet courtyard, the loud voices of an excited crowd of people greeted them on the street.

"I never knew there were so many people in the world," she said to her mistress. The procession came closer; several statues on platforms were being carried on the shoulders of men. "Who do those statues represent?" She took the risk of distracting her mistress with too many questions.

"These are the thunder gods that make rain come," she answered, not looking at her maid directly. "When they come by, bow down to them and pray to them, or the rain will not come."

The servant girl thought of the prophet Elisha and the warnings he made about false gods. In his scariest voice, he had held her spellbound in the village of Gilead when telling of the battle on Mt. Carmel between the prophets of Baal and Elijah, the prophet of the true God, Jehovah. Was she going to see this awful Baal who was called Hadad in Damascus? The true Jehovah caused the rains to come for Elijah.

Again she wished she knew how to write like Naaman. He made scratches on leather, which was rolled up and carried to faraway places. If she could write, she would have described this day to her family. She would also have tried to explain what she did and, to her regret, what she did not do. If only she really could write! She practiced an imaginary letter:

"The procession could be heard from a long ways off because of the loud drums and horns being blown. The wooden figures being carried before us were decorated with wreaths and flowers. The people began to shout and cry; many I am sure had been indulging in strong drink.

"Since I am small and my mistress was not paying attention to me, no one really noticed that I did not bow or pray to the idols, for that is what they were. Then I saw the biggest and most beautiful, the Anat, who is considered the wife of Hadad. This one was special because it was clothed.

"'Look at Anat,' my mistress shouted to me. 'Notice her dress; remember you made it. I am so proud of you; it is our special gift to the gods for today.' I could not believe my eyes, my knees grew weak, and I thought I would faint. I was terrified that my work had been dedicated to this false god without my knowledge. She thought I was bowing to this idol, but actually, I was trying to brace myself against fainting. I wish I had run away from this evil, but I was too weak to move. Dear true God of Israel, can you forgive me?"

She shuddered to think about what she had done. However, it got worse. She really had to tell someone, but did not dare confide with anyone in Damascus. She continued to write an imaginary letter to her family; it was the only option:

"Dear family, the whole crowd packed the streets and streamed to the Temple of Rimmon Hadad. Horrible bleating from a huge herd of terrified goats and sheep cut through the din of the crowd, and even drowned out the sound of beating drums. Yellow clouds of smoke sent intoxicating fumes into the air. I saw the bulging eyes of the animals, which trembled with fear in a corral where they were packed. Close to a huge alter already smoking with a crackling fire, I saw a priest grab a goat by a rear leg. Its struggle to escape was futile. He swung the animal over a stone table. The pathetic bleating stopped suddenly with a gurgle when the throat was slit by one deft movement of the priest.

"In a second, the goat hung limp and streams of blood flowed through troughs to a collecting basin. Still the marble floor of the temple was slick with blood. I was totally sick. Then I saw the huge image of Rimmon Hadad, a statue of a bull. Everyone was trying to shove their way forward to kiss its feet. I was supposed to also, but I pretended to take care of my lady's skirts to lift them out of the bloody muck."

THE SERVANT GIRL DARES

The Hebrew servant girl made it home by herself that day. No one seemed to notice how upset she was. Naaman's household just thought she was sick. "Dear God," she frequently prayed. "I know you are here with me in

The Servant Girl Who Boldly Witnessed

Damascus. I have not forgotten you. I know there is a reason for me to be here."

"Have you noticed that our master does not look well?" The servants were gossiping in the courtyard while they worked. "His skin has taken on a pale white color." Lately, Naaman had not been leaving to command battles as often.

"My husband, do you really have to leave again? You should take care of yourself and see doctors here in Damascus who can help you." The servant girl overheard a discussion between Naaman and his wife. The horrible word "leprosy" was whispered about the house. When she saw him again after another trip, it was obvious that something was terribly wrong. Many of the finest doctors of Damascus rushed silently across the courtyard to treat him with many bad smelling ointments. The flaky white patches grew larger, and he was tormented with itching.

She remembered the bald prophet Elisha who came through her village in Gilead regularly. The spellbinding stories he told about the events at the Sumerian palace were repeated for days after every visit. She shivered with fright at the memory of his warning about worshiping foreign gods who brought evil. Elisha preached about the one true God of Israel, and then he healed all kinds of diseases in the name of the great God, Jehovah!

"If only Master Naaman could travel to Elisha back home in Israel. Maybe he would be healed," she spoke in her excitement. "Wait! I am actually wishing for my enemy to get better!" She shocked herself to be thinking such thoughts.

"Send my master to visit the prophet who is in Israel! He could be healed of his leprosy," she pleaded with her mistress.

"Yes, we have tried everything else," her mistress relented. "Tell us more!"

"Praise God, they are listening to me." She thanked God as soon as she was alone. She was not used to people paying attention to her advice, but she had no doubt Elisha could heal.

"But how can you travel into the land of our enemy?" Naaman's wife considered every possible obstacle.

"The Hebrew servant girl from Gilead seems to be sure of herself, and we have tried everything else. We will find a way," Naaman said, determined to find a cure. The whole process required that he get a letter from the king of Syria to grant permission for him to go into the land of Israel. Technically, Israel was an enemy land. The household was in an uproar for the next several days. They loaded wagons with gifts to take to the servant girl's home country of Israel.

She did not tell them that Elisha would not be interested in the rich offerings of fine goods that they were taking to Israel, for he was more interested in what people thought and believed. But who was she to say anything? Maybe all of this wealth would come to some good. "To go to Israel!" She sobbed with tears rolling down her cheeks as the wagons rolled out of the courtyard. "Oh, if you see my family, tell them . . ." she suddenly remembered to shout, but it was too late. She was sure no one heard her.

Although she was certain of Elisha's healing abilities, she sometimes doubted if all the effort of the trip to Israel would turn out well. If not, would Naaman be angry with her? She trusted and prayed. Finally, Naaman and his entourage burst through the gates of the courtyard. He held the household spellbound with the story of his recovery, but they made the servant girl even more homesick, although she was happy for Naaman.

"Yes, I saw the Israelite prophet, Elisha. How amazing; he told me to bathe seven times in the Jordan River!" Naaman told the story over and over. "Now, we have amazingly clear rivers here in Damascus that are actually much less muddy than the Jordan. I don't understand what the difference could be." The servant girl knew that the power of the great Jehovah made the difference. "But this prophet Elisha, or rather the God of Israel whose prophet he is, preaches the true God." Naaman always added this remark as he told his story.

The Servant Girl Who Boldly Witnessed

"I wonder if he remembers who made the suggestion to him that he go to Israel for healing?" The servant girl wondered. She was quite desperate that Naaman would recall that she was the one who talked to his wife about Elisha. What she really hoped was that he remembered to tell Elisha about the Hebrew girl who worked in his household in Damascus.

At last, Naaman went to the servant girl. He hugged her so tightly that he lifted her right off the ground. She felt the skin of his arms, which were totally healed and smooth as the cheek of a baby. "My dear child," he said. "Elisha remembers you, a brave girl in Gilead who asked many questions and was absorbed in his stories. He was so sorry to hear that you were missing, but he was happy to hear everything about you and your witness to me. He is contacting your family immediately. They have moved back to your village."

She hung on to every bit of news from Israel.

"We will see about getting you back to Gilead as soon as arrangements can be made," Naaman added.

Her heart leaped. Most amazing of all, her master was a changed person because of the words of Elisha. He exclaimed to anyone who would listen that the God of Israel was the only true God. The servant girl gazed out of the second-floor window and was astonished by what she saw. "Why is a wagon parked in the courtyard heaped with a load of dirt?" she wondered. What kind of exchange was that for the treasures they took to Israel?

POINTS TO PONDER CONCERNING THE SERVANT GIRL WHO WITNESSED

A couple hundred years have passed since the reign of David. Like Miriam, from the book of Exodus, our main character here is a girl in a foreign land. Miriam was a Hebrew girl in the land of Egypt, but she was there with many thousands of people of her nationality. Egypt was the only home Miriam had ever known, for her people had lived there many centuries.

By contrast, this Hebrew girl is alone in the foreign land of Syria. The Bible does not tell us the whole story of how she came to be in Damascus. But we do know that her home country of Israel was constantly at war with many different surrounding lands, including Syria.

We can easily imagine that during one of those wars the enemy Syrians had overrun her village. Perhaps the rest of her family died or maybe they managed to escape into surrounding countryside. In this *Bold Girls* story, the servant girl was captured by the enemy. How frightful it must have been for her as foreign soldiers took her away to another land where the language, culture, and even the gods were different. Finally, after a long, terror-filled journey, the Hebrew girl found herself in a wealthy Syrian household as a servant.

As the Old Testament book of 2 Kings reveals, God watched over his little one. Her home in Syria belonged to Naaman, a military general for the king of Syria. Biblical passages hint that her existence in this household was tolerable. In any event, she must have been close to the family in order for Naaman, her powerful master, to listen to her advice to go to Israel for healing. Of course, she had thought often of her real family, their destiny, and if they would ever be reunited.

Living as a captive servant, or slave, in a foreign household has been the experience of many captives in war. Many people, especially children, have been kidnapped from their families and found themselves in situations not unlike the one described in this *Bold Girls* story. As portrayed, the main character has a fairly positive experience, but for many prisoners of war life is much worse. Such unfortunate captives might be happy to be alive, but they must adapt to a new culture in many ways. Many must also learn a new language and may even be forced to convert to the religion of their captors. If so, they face the difficult decision of how much to conform and when they must resist.

In the case of the Hebrew servant girl, she must have wondered if she would ever see the land of Israel again. But she never forgot her native land and she never forgot the one, true God she learned to love in her early childhood. She continued to worship him and obey him in the best way she could in a land of strangers.

Leprosy, or probably a skin disease like it, made the skin appear scaly white and was thought to resemble death. In Israel, the land of the servant girl's culture, people with visible skin disease were considered to be unclean and became social outcasts. However, despite the laws she had learned, the servant girl was not repulsed by the skin disease. Instead she thought about what she could do to help.

Who had helped her in the past? Of course, the God of Israel was with her wherever she went. The servant girl kept her faith in the God of Israel. His prophet Elisha often worked miracles in his name, and had healed people in the past. How amazing that Naaman, who was a rich and powerful

The Servant Girl Who Boldly Witnessed

man, took her suggestion, went to the land of his enemy, and eventually found Elisha!

God chooses unusual ways to work. Not always the strong but also the weak can work God's will. For example, the suggestion of a young servant girl caused Naaman to go to Elisha to be healed. When Elisha's way of healing seemed unlikely, Naaman asked, "What is wrong with the rivers of Damascus?" Naaman was ordered to bathe in the Jordan River seven times. He had expected to be healed in a much more dramatic manner! However, God does not always use important people or flashy ways to accomplish miracles. On this occasion, and many others, we will note in this series of *Bold Girls* stories that God chooses a girl to do the job.

During Naaman's stay in Israel, another servant came into the story and implored Naaman to follow Elisha's directions for healing to occur. Naaman reluctantly complied, and was indeed healed! He was so thankful he offered gifts to Elisha; but gifts were not what Elisha, God's prophet, wanted. Elisha wanted God to have the glory. And so, with great joy, Naaman said, "Now I know there is no God on earth, but the God of Israel."

This is a very important story for you to take to heart. You can make a difference, even if you do not consider yourself to be very talented or smart. Our servant girl, not unlike children throughout the ages, wanted to be helpful. This is a wonderful quality; do not lose this eagerness to come to the aid of those in trouble. Do not lose this "can do" attitude as you get older. Those of us who have been around a while have too often become "burned-out" from trying to do good.

Like Miriam, the Hebrew servant girl in Naaman's household had an idea. She used her head and then she used her mouth. She was not afraid to speak up, and she was not afraid to approach the mistress of the household with her idea. She was not ashamed of her God whom she had not forgotten in her years in a foreign land.

Naaman no doubt told everyone he met, for the rest of his life, about the miracle God performed for him. He is even mentioned in the New Testament, Luke 4:27. The servant girl is not heard from again in the Bible, although in this fictional version of the story she experiences a happy ending. She surely continued to tell of the God of Israel to whoever would listen. We would like to imagine that maybe one day she really did return to her native land, but this is unknown.

Why don't we learn her name? We will never know, but God knows her by her name. He who knows every sparrow is certain to know every child of his kingdom, even if her name is not recorded for us.

QUESTIONS FOR DISCUSSION

1. How did the servant girl remember her native culture and her true God, Jehovah, while living among strangers? What would you have done in the same situation?

2. The servant girl put on a cheerful, friendly attitude even though her heart was breaking. Would it have been more honest of her to be sullen and resentful of her misfortune? In that case, would she have accomplished God's mission for her?

3. Can you contrast the behavior of this girl with the children in Bethel? (See 2 Kings 2.) The same prophet, Elisha, encountered children on at least one other event in his travels and work. What happened on this occasion, and what can you learn from the incident?

4. Find the original passage for this *Bold Girls* story in 2 Kings 5. The complete story of how Naaman was healed takes up the whole chapter, but the mention of the servant girl occurs only in verses 2–4. Be sure to read these few verses and note how the story has been elaborated. Do you think that the imaginary items in this *Bold Girls* story are accurate historically? How would you imagine that a girl from Israel would find herself in the household of a Syrian army general? Your ideas about how this could have happened would be just as likely as this *Bold Girls* story, and may be even more interesting!

5. The scenes about the festival day in honor of Hadad are compiled from small pieces of information taken from many different sources, but was written mostly from imagination. Second Kings 5:12 mentions Damascus, so it is probably accurate to have this *Bold Girls* story take place in that ancient city.

6. Why did Naaman bring back a wagon full of soil from Israel? (See 2 Kings 5:17–18.)

The Servant Girl Who Boldly Witnessed

RELATED CULTURAL AND HISTORICAL QUESTIONS TO EXPLORE

1. Where can we find out how people worshipped false gods around the time of 825 bc in Damascus? The Bible itself tells us about the worship practices of ancient cultures, and how the Israelites often mixed up true worship of Yahweh with the worship of the surrounding cultures. Today, archaeological sites can be visited that give us an idea of the sites and buildings where false religions were practiced. Items can be seen in museums or in books about how the ancient Israelites built altars and temples to the true God.

   The idols and items used to worship false gods can also be seen. While many items have been found and ancient sites can be visited, the actual religious practices mostly remain unknown to us.

2. Second Kings 5:18 mentions a temple of Rimmon. Hardly anything is known of this temple, but the situation described in these verses is interesting. Sometime later, Naaman asks Elisha if he would be forgiven if he helps his master bow down in the temple of Rimmon, even though he himself now serves the true God of Israel. This is like the situation in the story that describes the servant girl on the pagan festival day. Without her knowledge, or in a circumstance beyond her control, she participates in the worship of the false god. Have you ever been in this situation, perhaps when you were visiting a friend and the family prayed to a different god or went to a different house of worship? What did you do?

3. Do such violent events occur in the lives of young people only in ancient times? Do such tragic things happen to children today? Does slavery still exist in the twenty-first century? Where are wars taking place right now? Are only soldiers affected by warfare?

SUGGESTED TOPICS OF DISCUSSION FOR TEACHERS AND PARENTS OF OLDER STUDENTS

1. The practices of pagan worship are interesting but often gruesome, including sacrifices and temple prostitution. Teenagers will find study of religion in ancient Near Eastern cultures to be challenging.

2. Why was Jezebel famous and what is the reason for her bad reputation? Why is a disreputable woman often called a "Jezebel"?

3. The ancient Israelites are not the only culture that sacrificed animals. Almost all the neighboring ancient Near East cultures practiced animal, and even human, sacrifices as part of their practice of religion. Why do you think sacrifices are such an important part of so many cultures? Have you ever killed an animal?

The Daughters Who Built the Walls of Jerusalem

Nehemiah 3:12

A RIDE IN THE RUINS

"The king of Persia, Artaxerxes, lives in glorious splendor and only drinks wine from golden goblets. However . . ." Nehemiah paused ominously, "he has many enemies. My job in Babylon as cupbearer was to taste the finest wine in the kingdom before the king drank it. It was a great job, unless someone had secretly slipped poison into the king's drink," Nehemiah confided. He was holding us spellbound with marvelous stories of faraway Mesopotamia.

"Well, did anyone ever do that?" I, the youngest of three sisters, innocently asked.

"I'm here, aren't I," Nehemiah said as he winked at me. My oldest sister kicked me under the table.

"Oh, I get it. If someone tried to poison Artaxerxes, you would have tasted the wine first, swallowed the poison, grabbed your throat, fallen to the floor, and you would be the dead person instead of the king!" I grasped my neck as I tried to imagine choking on a poison drink. My mother buried her face in her hands and Father shot me a warning glance.

"No, don't send the girls to their beds," he said to my parents. "It is wonderful to be your houseguest after living many years in the court of the Persian king." Nehemiah fell silent for a moment and sighed. "I have to share with you a secret God has laid on my heart. In Persia I wept and fasted when I heard how the stone walls of Jerusalem are still broken down and the wooden gates are burned. One day I brought wine to the king."

"After you tasted it?" I interrupted.

"Yes, after I tasted it." Then Nehemiah stood up straight and changed his voice to talk like the foreign king. "Why do you look so sad my good man, my cupbearer. You are normally so cheerful; are you sick?"

"I was very afraid," Nehemiah continued in his normal voice. "Here I was, a lowly cupbearer, in the presence of the king and queen, so I stammered, 'May the king live forever. Why shouldn't I be sad when the city of my ancestors is in ruins?'"

Returning to his kingly voice Nehemiah continued, "What is it you want?"

"I silently breathed a prayer to the God of Heaven, and then I took a deep breath before I answered the king." Nehemiah bobbed his head and clasped his hands together. "If it pleases the king and if your servant has found favor in his sight, let him send me to the city in Judah where my ancestors are buried so that I can rebuild it." Nehemiah seemed like a different man when he pretended to be the cupbearer.

"The king was favorably disposed to my request," Nehemiah said. "So here I am. I made this long trip to Jerusalem to organize the rebuilding of all the walls and gates that surround the city."

"We are poor people. We have no building materials, and hostile tribes in the countryside will prevent our every effort to rebuild our city," warned my grandfather, Hallohesh, who was one of the governors in Jerusalem. "The enemies of Judah are afraid we will grow strong again, and they want Jerusalem to remain weak."

"I've cried and I have prayed to God of heaven," Nehemiah said. "I reminded God of his promise to Moses, that even if his people are scattered, they will again be gathered together in the dwelling he has chosen. I prayed for success and the favor of the king for whom I served. I cannot deny this call. I am only a cupbearer; I don't know much about building walls and gates, but Jerusalem has lain in ruins for one hundred and thirty years, and I want to bring her back to her former beauty." Nehemiah picked up a stone and scratched a map of the city on our wooden tabletop. We sisters held our breath. Mother would surely protest when a guest scratched her table, but she seemed to be much more interested in what Nehemiah was describing to us. "I know I have to be careful. I have been here three days and have not seen anything of the damage yet. I need to get a good look and take a survey, but I don't want to arouse suspicion."

Then I took another small stone, and added more details to some sections of the wall. "The burned out Fountain Gate is here, but the path is real steep at this point, it is easy to slip and slide down the slope here. My sisters and I have explored the ruined walls our whole lives."

"Well, that can't be too many years my young friends," Nehemiah chuckled. "But you seem to know the terrain. The moon is shining tonight; come outside now and show me around. We will ride my horse." We were amazed at this unexpected opportunity and almost tripped each other in our haste to get out the door.

Mother started to protest, but Father and Grandfather were coming too. Honestly, they did not know the rubble like we sisters did. They needed us to keep them out of trouble, or they could fall into a cistern and break a leg.

The night was much darker than I expected when we got outside, but we certainly could not carry a torch. Nehemiah mounted his horse and let us take turns riding with him, but the horse could not make fast progress. Father, Grandfather, and my two sisters had no problems keeping up on foot.

"Yes, it is important that we are not noticed by those enemies who fiercely oppose any efforts to rebuild the city of Jerusalem," Nehemiah warned us.

"We need to hug the wall once we go outside the Valley Gate and stay hidden in the shadows." I whispered. We scrambled over heaps of rubble and clung to narrow paths. "Follow me to the Jackal's Well and be careful to not fall in. It is deep." We paused at the well and dropped some pebbles into it. They fell for a long time. We heard the faint echo come back when they hit the water. The horse seemed afraid of the narrow rocky path, especially after a small fox jumped out in front of us.

"Look at the Dung Gate," Nehemiah said. He shoved his shoulder against one of the double doors and tried to push it open. "The scorch marks are still visible and the hinges are rusty. Let this be a warning to us Jews. Yahweh allowed this severe judgment by the Babylonians for the disobedience of the Jews, but now by his grace he has caused the Babylonians to meet their own destruction. The Persians, who are allowing us to return from exile, now have conquered the Babylonians. I actually have a lot of materials already coming this way from the king of Persia," Nehemiah casually added. "I pray, and then I do."

"You what? . . ." my father, Shallum, stammered. "You already have lumber coming without even seeing the destruction first?"

"Yes, and by the way, the officials and priests don't know about any of this yet. Girls, help me keep this secret for as long as possible," Nehemiah warned us.

"What are you saying?" Grandfather did not believe his ears. "You have ordered up materials that will soon be delivered, without asking anyone for permission?"

"I have permission from a higher power. The gracious hand of Yahweh is upon me. I prayed; he answered. The king of Persia gave me letters for safe passage and here I am. The rest is just details," Nehemiah shrugged and smiled.

"Little details such as who will do the work . . . and what about our enemies who will fight us every step of the way?" my father asked. "The arrows will fly as soon as they see us start to work."

"The walls will encompass a smaller area than during the time of Hezekiah. The population is less now, but there are enough of us. The people of Jerusalem will come around," Nehemiah answered confidently. "They understand how vulnerable we are to attack and that we really need the fortifications. The Horonites and the Ammonites raid our gardens and vineyards at will."

"If every household contributed a few workers, it would be possible. What if every family rebuilt the portion of wall that is closest to their house?" my grandfather suggested. "Everyone wants to have a strong wall built up to protect their property."

"Now you are using your head," Nehemiah added.

Father sighed, "I only wish I had more men to help with the work."

"You send your daughters. The daughters of Shallum will be building walls, just you see," Nehemiah quickly answered. We stood silently in shocked excitement under the full moon while night creatures looked at us curiously from their dens.

"The City of David is beautiful even now in ruins, but can you imagine it all built up again?" I whispered to the others. "We want to help, Nehemiah, it is our dream, too."

"The God of heaven will give us success. Of course you will help."

THE ARROWS FLY

The secret was out only a few days later when construction materials started to arrive. We, the daughters of Shallum, were assigned a portion of the wall just like all the other families. Nearest our house was the section between the Tower of the Ovens and the Valley Gate. With Father, Grandfather, and other relatives, we worked from daybreak until evening while mother brought us food and water. Of course, we wanted our section of the wall to be strong and beautiful. We tried to imagine how the rocks fit together before the destruction by studying the pattern of how they fell. By using levers, we would pry them out of the dirt where they had become partially buried. We often found arrows from the attack long ago and sometimes even bones, which would be carefully gathered and buried elsewhere. We shuddered to think how the people who defended Jerusalem about 130 years ago had died.

We constructed scaffolding when the wall started getting taller than us. We rolled the rocks into a basket, which could be lifted high by a rope on a pulley. It was the hardest work that we had ever done, but when we paused and gazed across the city we felt blessed by Yahweh to see the walls of each section growing. Unfortunately, the quick progress of the first few days did not last. As Nehemiah had warned us, we started receiving angry words from the enemies who shouted at us from the valley.

"What are you feeble Jews doing?" we heard after about five days of work. "Will you bring the stones back to life from those heaps of rubble?" a few Ammonite boys taunted us. They thought that stones, which were blackened by the fires of the destruction, would crumble. We tested them all for soundness by striking them together. We had to reuse the stones from the rubble because we certainly did not have time to gather new stones.

Bold Girls Speak

They noticed that we were girls, the daughters of Shallum, and claimed, "Even a fox could break down that wall of stones by climbing on it." We shrugged our shoulders and ignored them at first, but then they started throwing rocks at us.

"Why don't they want us to rebuild the walls?" I asked my sisters.

"The Ammonites, the Arabs, and the Samarians are afraid that if the Jews become strong again, we will conquer their lands as well," my oldest sister answered. At about day ten, a few rocks rained down around us.

"Where are they falling from?" I looked up at the scaffolding where workers were hauling rocks. But they were being very careful and had not spilled any stones.

"They are coming from below. Watch out for that group of boys; they may have rocks in their hands to throw at us," my middle sister warned.

"Ouch, one hit me. That stung." I checked my leg.

"Isn't it enough that we have to lug rocks around? Now we also have to look over our shoulders constantly for unfamiliar bystanders who may not be friendly," my middle sister complained.

"We are weak people who have returned to our city after a long absence. We only want to rebuild what we once were given by Yahweh. How can they think we are strong enough to threaten them?" I said.

Nehemiah came around and encouraged us with a prayer, "Hear us, O our God, for we are despised. Turn their insults back on their own heads. Do not cover up their guilt, for they have thrown insults in the face of the builders." Nehemiah was one man who really could pray! We were working with all our heart and the walls were soon half as high as they would be when finished, and no gaps remained.

We were glad for the breaks when mother brought us food and drink. We would rest in the shade, but children gathered around who looked at

The Daughters Who Built the Walls of Jerusalem

our food with such hunger in their eyes. "I can't help it, I have to share with them," I said. Mother started adding extra food in the baskets, because she agreed that helping the poor is necessary and a good thing to do.

"Are they some of us; are they Israelites?" my middle sister asked. We started to talk to the grubby but polite children.

"We are Jews, too," they said in Aramaic. "We are from the country, but the farmers are suffering drought and our families can't harvest enough to feed us."

"Our father will sell us into slavery if we can't find food," they confided to us. "Thank you, our bellies are so empty." They happily left with bread and some olives.

"How is that possible that even our people can be so poor that they sell their own children?" We shuddered at the thought and discussed it with Nehemiah the next time he came around.

"Your mercy toward the poor is a special gift; thank you for telling me what you have learned," Nehemiah said thoughtfully. He had recently become a very important governor because of his leadership of the rebuilding project. "Some of our people are rich, but most are very poor. When the poor need money, they have to ask the rich for a loan. But the rich also add on unfair interest. When the poor cannot pay it, they have to turn to desperate measures. You have made me aware of how necessary it is to make new laws against this unfairness," Nehemiah said. He was angry now.

"Why are new laws always necessary; can't more people just share?" I asked. Nehemiah just sighed and seemed to sink into further thought.

In addition to these problems among our own people, we saw more enemies creeping up the slope to the walls. After about twenty days of building, we saw men of military age carrying swords and bows. To slow their progress, we rolled rocks down into the valley, which would start a small avalanche. That at least distracted the enemy; we had plenty of rocks. So many problems; for every step forward, new obstacles stood in our path. The builders were getting weary, and we thought we would never see the bottom of the rubble. In addition, the poor children showed up regularly.

"You know they are plotting against you," they confided to us. "Wherever you turn, they will attack." We gave the children food and continued to talk to them. They trusted us, maybe because we were young women. We also discovered that they had ways to find out information, especially since most people just considered them to be poor beggars; even the enemies paid them no attention. They shared what they knew with us. "The enemies will try to get in behind the walls. They will try to kill you and put a stop to the work," they told us one day. We found them to be trustworthy, and so we carefully listened to their news and passed it along.

By day thirty, arrows almost reached us several times. It was hard to keep our attention on the work, knowing that at any moment the enemy may attack. My sisters and I became good with slings; we always had hunted birds to add to the cooking pot before the building began, but now we became much better shots. At least we gave some of the enemy a headache.

"Don't be afraid, we are not working on our own strength. Yahweh is great and awesome; he will give us wisdom," Nehemiah assured us. "We pray to our God and then we post guards to watch day and night." Now everyone had to work with one hand holding a shield and the other laying stones. Soldiers were placed at regular intervals along the wall, but there were not enough of us to be stretched so thin. If we heard a trumpet, we had to run to that area to help out.

After about forty days of building, the enemies noted our determination and finally lost their confidence to harass us. They realized that this work had been done with the help of our God, so they left us to build in peace and we made good progress. The other matter, the poverty of so many of our people, persisted. We continued to talk to Nehemiah and he grew very angry about our, and others, reports. He called a large meeting that included the nobles and officials. My sisters and I had never seen such a large gathering of the people of Jerusalem.

"What you are doing is not right!" Nehemiah shouted. He always said exactly what he meant. We had never seen him so angry, and he was not afraid to stand up to the powerful and wealthy. "Shouldn't you walk in the fear of our God? What kind of impression does your lack of concern for the poor make on our Gentile enemies? Give back to the people the vineyards, fields, olive groves, and houses which you have taken unfairly."

"We will give it back, and not demand anything more from them. We will do as you say," the wealthy people said. And then they took an oath. We were amazed at their compliance; Yahweh was working in them to do right. Truly, it was again more evidence of God's power.

Nehemiah continued in his usual dramatic fashion by shaking his robe as though to empty his pockets. "See I am holding nothing back. Since I have been governor, I have not taken any wages. I share my wealth, and I loan money without charging interest. Remember me with favor, O my God, for all I have done for these people."

THE ENEMY PERSISTS

Because of our relationship with the poor children who continued to come around for food, we got wind of a plot that would have put Nehemiah in danger yet again. "Be careful; the enemies want Nehemiah to meet them outside of Jerusalem, but they really mean to harm him," the children told us. We told Nehemiah what we had heard. We did not know how Jerusalem could have been rebuilt without him, and it seemed that our enemies were still not content to leave us in peace.

One evening Nehemiah hurried into our house and collapsed at our table. "The hand of Yahweh protected me this night, just as he has so many times." We were always anxious to hear Nehemiah's stories. He was blessed by Yahweh with wisdom and vision. "I received a message from Sanballat and Geshem, the enemies. They said, 'Come let us meet together in one of the villages on the plain of Ono.'" Nehemiah drew a map on our table, which by now was well scratched by Nehemiah's stories. "Well my suspicions were up because of what the girls told me. Four times these enemies sent me that message."

"The enemy just doesn't give up," my father added. "What have they tried now?"

"I sent a message to them saying that I cannot leave my people to do the work while I go to talk to them," Nehemiah replied. "They still did not give up. The fifth time the enemies said, 'You are going to declare yourself king of Judah and then lead a revolt against the king of Babylon. We will all be in danger because of you,' they claimed."

"You, a king? Come on, you would never make yourself a king," I said.

"You know me very well, my girl," Nehemiah said. "I told them bluntly, 'Nothing like what you are saying is happening; you are just making it up out of your head.'"

"Yes, they have very strange things in their heads," I could not help adding.

"Now let me finish," Nehemiah said. He was momentarily perturbed at me. "I told them, 'You are just trying to frighten us. You think our hands will become too weak to finish the walls, but I pray to Yahweh to strengthen our hands.' But that wasn't the end. Sanballat sent me a new message telling me that I should go to the temple and shut the doors to save my life because that very night enemies were going to kill me."

We were on the edge of our seats.

"You didn't trust that message did you?" my father asked. I was glad he had spoken so that I did not have to interrupt again.

"No," Nehemiah continued. "Should someone like me run away? Should one like me go into the temple to save his life? 'I will not go!' I told them."

"Praise Yahweh that he gave you the insight to realize this was a plot to get you alone, locked in the temple to kill you," my grandfather added.

"And praise Yahweh I have been getting some hints from the underground," Nehemiah patted my hand.

Nehemiah's courage gave us courage to continue. We recognized his qualities as a great leader and learned from his example. Other young people, as well as old, were working on the walls with us. We were the only girls, and we may have been smaller than the others, but we discovered ways of doing things with less strength. We noted ways of laying the stones in a beautiful pattern around the gates. We also learned to pray for strength as Nehemiah prayed. We felt God's will that we do this.

After fifty-two days the walls were built up to the former height and the gates were set in. The walls were sturdy and the gold-hued limestone of Jerusalem glowed warmly in the light of the setting sun. Inside the walls, new houses were being rebuilt, but still much of the space enclosed by the walls was vacant.

MEETING THE ENEMY

On the first day of the seventh month, Ezra, who was a teacher well versed in the law of Moses, started to plan a big dedication ceremony. He had been in Jerusalem even longer than Nehemiah. He decided to have a great celebration when the walls were completed and ready to be dedicated.

The city was alive with new energy after fifty-two days of hard labor. Many people from the countryside came into the city, and we all stood before the Water Gate. Ezra read the book of the law of Moses from daybreak until noon to all the women, men, and children who could understand. A high wooden platform was built for Ezra to stand on, so we could all see and hear as he began with praise to God. All the people lifted their hands and shouted, "Amen Amen!"

I was excited to hear the law of Moses as it was written. We had no scrolls and few people could read, not even most men and certainly none of the women. Only the priests could read, and we did not know how they, or anyone else, learned to read. It was kind of a miracle to be able to hear the very words of Moses, which he wrote many hundreds of years earlier after the exodus from Egypt. We listened attentively even though we stood long hours while the sun moved from low in the east to directly overhead. We were thankful for good understanding, because Ezra explained everything so well. Amazingly, new laws were discovered as a result of this reading, laws that the people had forgotten over the years. Waves of weeping spread across the crowd. We were so sorry that certain of Yahweh's laws were not being kept because they were unknown. We were afraid that Yahweh was angry about these laws that Moses had written but we did not obey.

Nehemiah, Ezra, and the priests noticed the people weeping and instructed, "This day is sacred to the Lord your God. Be still and do not grieve." Nehemiah said, "Go and enjoy choice food and sweet drinks, and send some to those who have nothing prepared. This day is sacred to our Lord. Do not grieve, for the joy of the Lord is your strength." We were all very glad to hear these words and dried our tears.

By reading the law publically, we also had discovered a new holiday that had not been celebrated since the days of Joshua. Ezra had read from the law of Moses, "The Israelites are to live in booths during the feast of the seventh month, and they should proclaim this word and spread it throughout their towns and in Jerusalem. Go out into the hill country and bring back branches from wild olive trees, and from myrtles, palms, and shade trees, to make booths. Then live in these temporary houses for seven days."

We sisters enthusiastically got involved with the preparations. After all the building we had done on the walls recently, building a booth was going to be no challenge at all, so we thought. Because our enemies had been quiet, we were able to wander away from the walls of Jerusalem for the first time in a couple months, since before the walls had been rebuilt. Also, the vegetation closely surrounding Jerusalem was very sparse and needed to be regrown. We wandered quite a long ways into the hill country to find large braches to build a small house for the celebration of the seventh month. It was quite an excursion. We had our donkey with us to carry branches, along with some food, axes, knives, and our slings in case a nice quail showed up. A good shot meant we could surprise mother with meat for a stew.

We were sizing up trees to find some good straight poles when we heard voices and rustling just out of our sight. "Are they friendly or enemies? Do we freeze and hope they pass by and not notice us? Do we climb up a tree and hide? No, they will steal our donkey." We quickly gathered some stones and had our slings ready in our hands.

"Hey look behind the trees, there are the sisters that were building the walls of Jerusalem," a young voice said. A group of Ammonite boys appeared. "Watch out, they are armed with those formidable weapons," one boy said. There was no escaping now. "Come on girls, we mean no harm." The Ammonite boys approached us cautiously, but they kept a close eye on our slings. I am sure they would have retreated if we had lobbed a rock in their direction.

We slowly put down our slings. "What are you doing?" one asked. "You have sure put a load of wood on that donkey."

"We are gathering logs and branches to build a booth," my oldest sister answered.

"Well whatever for? Certainly you Israelites don't need to build such a flimsy house out of wood. You have made the stones come alive from the ruins; you can build houses out of rocks."

"And they are strong enough that a fox can't knock them over," another boy said. We now knew these were the same boys who had taunted us earlier.

"It is to fulfill a new command, I mean an old command that was just discovered from the time of Moses," my middle sister said. "For the feast of

The Daughters Who Built the Walls of Jerusalem

the seventh month we are to build a small house to live in for seven days to remember the time of wandering in the wilderness and celebrate the delivery of the Jews from Egypt by Yahweh."

"We Ammonites have heard that among the laws discovered it is stated that neither Ammonites nor Moabites should ever be admitted into the assembly at the temple," one boy said. We were surprised that they were so well informed.

"Yes, because during the time long ago of the wandering in the wilderness, the Ammonites and Moabites did not help us in our travels by offering food and water. Instead, the king of Moab, Balak, hired the magician Balaam to speak against Israel. But because Yahweh put words into his mouth, Balaam spoke blessings instead." I could easily remember the story about the donkey that talked.

"So because of something that happened so long ago, we are being excluded?" one boy asked. "That hardly seems fair." I must admit . . . I did not know how to answer that.

"Well, you still reject our God, Yahweh, and you tried to prevent us from rebuilding the walls. In fact, an Ammonite tried to kill Nehemiah several times. Come with us back to Jerusalem and see how we build the booth for this celebration," my oldest sister invited them. I hoped she knew what she was doing.

With no problems at all, we built the small house on the flat roof of our house where we normally spent hot summer evenings. For seven days we primarily lived up there, had our meals outside, and spent time talking about the history of the Israelites. We talked especially about the time in the wilderness, and we celebrated our deliverance and protection by the hand of Yahweh from Egypt. The Ammonite boys came up one evening; Grandfather was not at all upset with us.

"It is right and good that the Ammonites are with us, because part of the law says, as Moses wrote it and Ezra read it, we are 'to live in booths during the feast of the seventh month, and we should proclaim this word and spread it throughout the towns and in Jerusalem.' All of our neighbors and even our enemies should know about this custom and our history," Grandfather explained. "We are glad to share with you our food and our traditions."

"Well, maybe you are not really so keen to take over all the land and drive us out," one of the boys said. Our former adversaries were becoming slowly convinced of our good intentions. "We like your custom of living in little houses for seven days, and your food as well."

"There is something that even my granddaughters do not know," Grandfather continued. My parents glanced at each other uncomfortably. "Nehemiah has just repeated a law that Ezra had enforced very strictly a couple generations ago. No Israelites are to marry foreign wives. At that time your grandmother and I were young and had just married." We had never seen Grandfather with tears in his eyes. "Of course you girls don't remember your grandmother; she died before you were born. Ezra commanded back then that even if we were already married, all foreign wives had to be deserted. Well, your grandmother was an Ammonite, but there is no way I was going to desert her. She had become a believer in Yahweh, just like other foreigners have become believers, like Ruth and Rehab. So you see, Granddaughters, you also have foreign blood."

This was new information but did not really change anything concerning us. Our friends and family were the same. However, we now saw our enemies in a different light.

CELEBRATION OF A NEW JERUSALEM

Priests from the tribe of Levi were brought to Jerusalem to lead the dedication of the walls. New music-making objects appeared that we had never imagined before—cymbals, harps, and lyres. What marvelous new sounds we heard. Along with professional singers, the youth were also asked to sing. Not since the days of David, who had a choir director named Asaph, did Israel have a choir director. The priests and Levites purified themselves, and then they purified the people, the gates, and the wall. It was an exciting morning when we gathered at the pool at the lowest corner of Jerusalem with all the other singers. We climbed the broad steps to the temple. The column of singers split into two directions, one row climbing stairs off to the right and the other to the left. On the top of the wall, the two choirs together sang to create a wonderful sound of thanksgiving to Yahweh. Some songs we sang back and forth with the other group so the music echoed off the walls. We sang louder than we had ever sung before. I think we were mostly on the correct pitch with the rest of the choir. Just when the sound could not be more magnificent, trumpets joined us. The rejoicing could be heard for a great distance into the countryside. We felt tremors in our knees and voices as we looked over the city from the walls that we had helped

The Daughters Who Built the Walls of Jerusalem

build. At the end of the last note, we all stood silently until the last sound disappeared in the distant mountains.

"Yahweh, did you hear our worship; are you pleased?" we asked.

We were sure Yahweh heard.

POINTS TO PONDER ABOUT THE DAUGHTERS WHO BUILT

This whole story is built on only one verse from Nehemiah 3:12: "Shallum son of Hallohesh, ruler of a half-district of Jerusalem, repaired the next section with the help of his daughters." Chapter three of Nehemiah lists the many families who had a section of wall to rebuild, and the sons are mentioned as workers. I found it fascinating that out of the entire list of sons, only in the last verse where offspring are listed, verse 12, is Shallum and his daughters mentioned. I wondered what the story was behind just that one verse. We really do not even know how many daughters were in this family, meaning that the details of this *Bold Girls* story are fictional. Even so, the entire book of Nehemiah offers many historical details to build upon. Ultimately, this story really is Nehemiah's. He was a very unusual character, and he exemplifies many admirable qualities from which we can learn.

Why was Jerusalem in ruins? Be sure to look up the recent history of the Israelites in exile. The life of a family with daughters and no sons could be similar to this imaginative *Bold Girls* story. Sons are always mentioned as a blessing, but many daughters were often seen as a liability. Hints are given that this type of situation was not always true, and the mere mention of daughters building at this time of Jerusalem's history shows that they also took up their share of the work and responsibility.

This *Bold Girls* story features many authentic issues that were occurring during this time. Israel did have many enemies that resisted the rebuilding of the walls of Jerusalem, and the taunts that harassed the builders in this story are taken from the Nehemiah text. Another authentic issue was the exploitation of the poor by the rich. It is true that many people were so close to starvation that they had to sell their children. Nehemiah was such an effective leader that he managed to make new laws to improve the living circumstances of the poor. It is also true that the old laws were rediscovered and Ezra put them into effect. Intermarriage with non-Israelites was a problem because it brought in pagan customs. The book of Nehemiah also describes the dedication of the wall as a big celebration, which this *Bold*

Girls story has tried to recreate. Each of these issues is worth a good discussion. The disparity between the rich and the poor, as well as our relationships with our enemies, are issues that remain with us today.

Be sure to read the book of Nehemiah. It gives a vivid glimpse into how practical problems were solved at that difficult time. This *Bold Girls* story follows the events of the book of Nehemiah, and much conversation is taken right from the pages of the Old Testament. Be sure to note the parts of this story that are quoted from the book of Nehemiah and the parts that are fictional additions. Also, note the Jews' total dependence on God's help every step of the way to guide them in finding solutions to every challenge.

QUESTIONS FOR DISCUSSION

1. Look up Nehemiah 6:15. In how many days did they rebuild the wall? What problems did they encounter?
2. Read Nehemiah's prayer in Nehemiah 1:5–11. Why is it such a powerful example of prayer?
3. How could Nehemiah be so sure of what God willed him to do?
4. What kind of leader was Nehemiah? How did he set a good example before the people?
5. Why did some people live in poverty? What did Nehemiah do about it? Does this problem exist today?

RELATED CULTURAL AND HISTORICAL QUESTIONS TO EXPLORE

1. How were laws made at that time? How would you classify this kind of government? How does the government of Jerusalem differ from the government of other countries of that time? Of today?
2. These sisters may have had extra privileges because they were the daughters of a ruler in Jerusalem. Could they have taken advantage of their status to avoid the hard, dirty, and dangerous work?
3. Should there be rules about different kinds of work for boys and girls? Why or why not?
4. How can you help people who do not have enough to eat?

SUGGESTED TOPICS OF DISCUSSION FOR TEACHERS AND PARENTS OF OLDER STUDENTS

1. Discuss the advantages or difficulties of marriage between people of different nationalities and different religions.

The Girl Whose Hand Jesus Touched

MATTHEW 9:18–25; MARK 5:21–43; LUKE 8:40–56

A VISION ON THE WATER

"Keep your eye on the wharf of Capernaum. Am I oaring straight or in circles?" My boat seemed to make little progress against the waves.

"I'm trying to see, but it is getting dark and the rain is picking up," Petra strained her eyes to the north. "We should have come in sooner, but the fishing was so good."

"I sure hope our parents will be distracted by how many fish we caught instead of how late we stayed out," I added.

"If we get back before dark—if we get back at all—we are starting to take on water," Petra betrayed panic in her voice.

My friend and I had gone out on the Sea of Galilee for the afternoon to do what we like to do best: fish. It started out as a beautiful day with little waves, and the fish were biting. We forgot the time and drifted beyond sight of Capernaum. Likewise, the sun had moved across the sky faster than we realized.

"Are we getting any closer?" No answer. "Can you see the wharf?" I asked louder.

"Well, sort of," Petra replied. That did not sound good at all.

Terror was setting in and the wind was strong—not in our favor. We both took an oar, coordinated our strokes, and rowed against the wind with all our strength, hopefully due north. We did not have enough breath to talk in detail about our dire situation.

"What is that ahead of us?" I asked.

"Where?" Our oars stopped midair.

The Girl Whose Hand Jesus Touched

"On the water. Is it a boat with a sail? Or is it some sort of mirage," I pointed.

"Yes, I see it too—a figure, a person—no, an angel," Petra hesitated.

"It is a being of some kind, and it recognizes us," I was too amazed to be scared.

"He, yes it looks like a man, is motioning us to follow," Petra noted.

"The wind has changed direction in our favor," I exclaimed with relief.

"We are being swept toward Capernaum," Petra was encouraged.

We seemed to fly north with the waves. In no time, the wharf was clearly in sight. The wind suddenly died down, and we reached shore. Enough light remained to divide our fish into two baskets, and we each nervously headed to our own houses.

"Didn't you notice it getting dark?" my mother greeted me. "Your father and I were just beginning to worry."

"Yes, Mother, sorry. Wasn't there a bit of a squall here in the village?" Mother looked at me quizzically. "Never mind, look at the nice fish we caught." I thought it better not to mention the storm on the lake, and I certainly was not going to talk about the other event.

Mother appraised the fish with a critical eye. "Yes, nice tilapia, we will prepare them tomorrow for Sabbath the next day."

Later I discovered that, apparently, the wind and the rain had not reached the village. That was one miracle, and then there was the other. I could not shake the memory of the figure on the lake.

The next morning I caught up with my fishing friend, Petra.

"What did your parents say when you came back late?" I asked.

"Actually, not much," Petra seemed preoccupied. "My grandmother is ailing, so they are distracted, and there is extra work at the house."

"Have you mentioned to anyone what we saw on the water?" I asked.

"No, but I can't get it out of my mind," Petra answered. "We have a house guest, a friend of my father's, so I have to get those fish we caught last night cleaned. I will see you at the synagogue on the Sabbath."

This eve of Sabbath, like all others, was filled with preparations. In late summer at the market in Capernaum, the selection brought in by the farmers is good, and I purchased goat cheese and melons. I did not need to look at the fish; we had plenty for Sabbath dinner. I took the long way back to the house to check if anything new was happening at the wharf. Boats of all shapes were unloading goods in the small harbor. I noted the passengers who had arrived, including Roman soldiers from all over the Empire who serve at the garrison located near Capernaum. At sundown, Sabbath begins and all preparations have to be complete. Fishermen come in early off the lake to unload their haul and hang their nets to dry while the sun is still high in the west. Everyone has a relaxed, festive mood on Sabbath eve because the workweek is over.

One boat that attracted my eye was the source of an unusual amount of laughter and splashing. The fishermen were stripped down, like they often do when fishing, and they were jumping off the boat for a good rinse-off in the fresh warm water of the Sea of Galilee. When I got closer, I noticed one was Petra's father, Simon, and Petra's unmarried uncle, Andrew. They lived in quite a large house that was always lively and fun. Our house was much quieter because I was an only child. Another pair of brothers was also with the group, John and James Zebedee, younger men in their early twenties. I did not recognize the fifth man. When they noticed me watching them, Petra's father waved at me and I waved back. With a half-hearted attempt at modesty, they paused with their feet on the lake bottom. They remained standing in the neck-high water until I passed; then the splashing resumed. I hurried on home with my purchases to help mother.

Too soon, the sun set behind the western hills marking the beginning of Sabbath. My father, mother, and I gathered at the table. With us were also some guests from other areas of Galilee. On the Sabbath no traveling is allowed. Since my father, Jairus, is the chief caretaker of the synagogue of Capernaum, we often had extra people at the table. I only half listened to the conversation of the adults; really I was trying to stay awake. They commented on the delicious fish, and remarked how lovely it would be to live by the lake. My ears perked up when a guest began discussing the miraculous works of a man from Nazareth whom he had seen in the area. He described how this man, named Jesus, is able to heal people who had all kinds of ailments. He said that Jesus was an exceptional rabbi as well, but he did not know where Jesus had studied. Quite frequently, we hear about traveling miracle workers around the lake, and they all turn out to be charlatans. I excused myself as soon as it was polite and quickly slipped away so that I could go to sleep.

Capernaum becomes very still on the Sabbath; we eat nothing in the morning and quietly walk the short distance to the synagogue. We sit on backless, stone benches around the perimeter of the building. I waved to Petra before the rabbi came in and took his place in front of the Torah ark, which contained the sacred scrolls. The congregation joined with the local rabbi in repeating prayers, and he read a passage from the Torah.

A new rabbi was handed a scroll. He quickly found a specific passage and read fluently from Isaiah 61 in Hebrew: "The Spirit of the sovereign Lord is on me, because the Lord has anointed me to preach good news to the poor."

"Today this Scripture is fulfilled in your hearing," he said, and then put down the scroll.

The congregation collectively drew in their breath. Comments and questions quickly filled the room with excited chatter, "How dare this newcomer, a relatively young, unknown rabbi make this claim? Who is he?" they all asked.

"He is Jesus, from Nazareth, his father is a carpenter, and Mary is his mother," the people said, trying to make sense of his ancestry.

"Is he claiming to be the Messiah who will deliver the Jews from the Romans and restore Israel?" The conversation became agitated.

Suddenly, a disheveled man leaped out into the open space in the middle of the room and shouted, "What do you want with us, Jesus of Nazareth? Have you come to destroy us? I know who you are —the Holy One of God!"

"Be quiet," Jesus said sternly. "Come out of him!"

The man shrieked in utter agony and was flung violently to the floor by an invisible force.

"What is going on?" we all asked each other. "What is this? A new teaching . . . and with authority! He even gives orders to evil spirits and they obey him."

Mother, Father, with our guests, walked home. All the while they discussed the strange event and its meaning. My father, who was well informed, said, "Unclean spirits call their opposites by name in order to gain control. This spirit called him 'the Holy One of God.' Therefore we know that the unclean spirit is the opposite of God's Spirit."

They thought about what my father had said and further analyzed the event. "Jesus is destroying evil in the world as we would expect the Messiah to do. Remember what John the Baptist said, 'The kingdom of heaven is near?' Has the time really come?"

WHO IS THIS MAN?

Later in the afternoon, I walked over to Petra's house. I really wanted to see her. So many events had occurred lately—so much to discuss! The normally busy household was subdued. Her grandmother was sick with a fever, and it was quickly becoming much worse. The usual remedies were not effective; the only hope remaining for her was a miracle. I sat down quietly with Petra by her grandmother's bed and prayed with her. Her grandmother did not seem to be aware of our presence.

Her sons, Simon and Andrew, quietly entered into the room. The other fishermen, James and John, joined us with the new rabbi who had spoken that morning, Jesus. I was surprised this man was the houseguest Petra had mentioned. He walked directly over to the bedside, bent over, and told the fever to leave. It was like the miracle in the synagogue. He performed none of the expected fancy incantations, magic potions, or secret signs. He just commanded the fever to leave. Yes, he did indeed heal with authority! Then he took her hand and helped her up from the bed.

Petra and her family were overjoyed. They praised God and thanked Jesus. Petra hugged her grandmother who spryly got up and started bustling about to take care of everyone, which was her greatest pleasure.

I could not begin to explain it; two miracles in one day. Seeing the event this morning was impressive, but once is not enough to convince me. Now it had happened again. This man, Jesus, has special powers. He uses his power for good, to destroy evil spirits and sickness. Is this the breaking in of the "new kingdom," which will be free of disease and unclean spirits?

When we finally met up a few days later, Petra reported her grandmother was doing better than ever. We discussed the latest events while skipping stones over the lake.

"I wonder about this new rabbi, Jesus," I shared with Petra. "I am happy, of course, that he cures those who are ill, but he did it on the Sabbath. Would a true Jew do that?" I asked.

"He cured my grandmother, that is convincing enough for me," said Petra.

"Maybe the new kingdom is really come—Israel will again reign—my father is totally convinced," Petra added.

"But can he be the Messiah for whom our people have waited for a very long time?" I continued. "It will be wonderful; this will be the time when Satan is defeated, sickness and nature are conquered, and the mighty are brought low."

The Girl Whose Hand Jesus Touched

"Jesus is surely attracting a lot of attention," Petra said. "When he is in town, the place is full of people clamoring to be healed by him, and they gather in our house. I can't keep the floor swept." We enjoyed the rare break, and were grateful for the time together, just being friends.

"Have you thought more about our fishing adventure?' I asked as we reluctantly left the shore.

"Yes, I shudder at the memory—we were almost lost—and what was that we saw?" Petra wondered.

"A guardian angel for sure," we agreed.

"What is on the roof of your house?" I asked after we turned toward the village.

"I can't believe my eyes. Four people are up there and they seem to be tearing the roof apart. I am not sure the roof can hold that much weight. It is only made of mud and waddle. I have to get back home . . . let's see what is going on," Petra urged. "Jesus must be back in the village. Are people so anxious to see him that they need to wreck the house?"

We rushed up the road. When we arrived, we found that the front courtyard was packed with a crowd.

"The whole village is here, straining to see whatever is going on; I can't get into my own house," Petra said. "Come around in the back; we can climb over the wall and get in through a window." She knew where the toeholds were worn in the cracks between the black basalt bricks. We managed to claw over the wall that was twice higher than we were tall, and jumped into the garden.

We scrambled through the back window just in time to hear, "Son, your sins are forgiven." A man was lying very still on a mat, and apparently unable to move. He was illuminated in a spot of sunlight that lit up the normally dark room.

"Well, the man has problems moving. If Jesus can heal, then he should heal him. Why is Jesus talking about forgiving sins?" I whispered to Petra.

Some teachers of the law were looking rather undignified, covered with dust on their heads and shoulders, mumbling among themselves. "Why does this fellow talk like that? He's blaspheming! Who can forgive sins but God alone?"

"That is only possible by the actions of the priests and the temple," I nudged Petra. "How can he be greater than the temple?"

"Why are you thinking these things?" Jesus interrupted my thoughts, and continued, "Which is easier: to say to the paralytic, 'Your sins are forgiven,' or to say, 'Get up, take your mat and walk'? But that you may know that the Son of Man has authority on earth to forgive sins."

"Is Jesus talking to me? That is exactly what I was thinking," my heart skipped a beat. "Does he know what I was just thinking?" I gulped.

Praise God that Jesus apparently was talking to the Pharisees. Jesus did not appear to be occupied with my thoughts at just that moment.

Jesus commanded the paralytic, "I tell you, get up, take your mat and go home." The motionless man suddenly sat up. He steadily put one foot ahead of the other, and rolled up his mat. The crowd that was gathered tightly around him stepped back to form a path for him to walk out of the house. His four friends, who had lowered him through the hole in the roof, rejoiced and followed quickly after him.

"Praise God for this miracle!" Petra joined with all the rest of the crowd.

In a few minutes, the sun was setting, the house was empty, and the crowd, full of praise, was out in the street. More people were clambering around Jesus with pleas for various kinds of healing.

"Now we need another miracle," Petra said. She, along with her mother and grandmother, remained behind looking up through the hole in the ceiling of their front room.

IN THE BOAT AGAIN

Some time had passed before Petra and I got together again for our favorite activity, which was to take out my small boat and talk about events. This time we brought along nets to catch sardines. We drifted near the shore to the south of Capernaum.

"It has been a mad house at our place with Jesus coming in and out. When he and my father and Uncle Andrew are in the house, crowds of people hardly let him have time to eat. Jesus' family came to our house a few days ago."

"Is your roof repaired?" I asked.

"Oh, yes. It was rather nice open, but of course, winter will come," Petra continued. "Wait until I tell you the latest. This is scary."

"I like scary," I encouraged her.

"More like eerie. Remember the last time when we were on the water?" Petra asked.

"How could I ever forget?"

The Girl Whose Hand Jesus Touched

"Last night, my father and the other men who have been following Jesus were out in our big boat and they were in the middle of the lake. A storm came up, just like that other time when we were out," Petra said.

"Did it storm last night? I must have slept through it." I really had not noticed.

"As my father tells it, the waves were crashing over the boat and it was beginning to fill. Can you believe that Jesus stayed underneath in the cabin and was sleeping? He didn't even wake up," Petra continued.

"Well, the people are bothering him so much, he must really be tired," I said.

"Sleeping through a storm? The men woke him up and asked, 'Teacher, don't you care if we drown?' From what my father said, he was rather upset that they disturbed his sleep," Petra continued.

"Jesus sometimes just seems like a regular guy, like when I saw them swimming. But other times he is really supernatural," I observed.

"Jesus stood on deck and simply shouted to the wind, 'Quiet! Be still!' and then the wind was still," Petra said. "Just like that. The wind obeyed him."

"He can make illness go away, demand unclean spirits to leave, and command the wind to stop. So, who is he really?" I asked, not expecting an answer.

"That is something like what happened to us on the water. One minute we were in danger, and then the next minute the wind shifted and just blew us home. Do you suppose he was on the water that evening?" Petra tentatively suggested.

Something caught my eye. "Look at the crowd on shore," I interrupted. "People are gathered in the small harbor."

"Jesus must be back again. Let's go over there and watch from the water. Something always happens when Jesus is around," Petra suggested. We headed toward shallow water.

A voice shouted to us, "Daughters, I know you are handy with a boat, come on over and help me out."

"Who? Us?" I asked.

"It is Jesus, the people are crowding him so tightly, he is standing in the water," Petra said. "How does he know about our ability with boats?"

"We are coming," I shouted to Jesus. He was wading in the water toward us. We made a few oar strokes, and he was at our starboard side. He easily reached across the boat, grabbed both sides, and lifted himself gracefully into the boat.

"Careful! Don't stand in the boat . . . oh, never mind," I realized my warning was ridiculous. Jesus seemed to defy the rocking motion of the boat and stood very securely upright. He remained standing while he directed us to row a few strokes farther from shore and drop the anchor overboard.

"Listen! A farmer went out to sow his seed. As he was scattering the seed, some fell along the path . . ." Jesus spoke wonderful words. He called his stories parables; at first hearing some of them were not easy to understand.

"What shall we say the kingdom of heaven is like? It is like a mustard seed, which is the smallest seed, yet when planted, it grows and becomes the largest plant," Jesus continued. That sounded like a good idea to us; we were little people.

"Do you bring in a lamp to put it under a bowl or a bed? Instead, don't you put it on its stand?" Jesus held us spellbound. Now this parable was not hard to understand. Time stood still, soon the sun faded in the west. Jesus said a benediction and dismissed the crowd, which reluctantly turned away. We turned from shore and headed the short distance back to Capernaum. Jesus finally sat down exhausted in the boat. He turned to us.

"Simon's daughter," he addressed Petra, "I hope your sardines didn't spoil in the sun. Take me to your house and let's fry them in oil and pour some of your father's good wine." Jesus seemed to think he was entitled to other people's food. Well, I suppose if he asks unclean spirits to leave, he can ask for his supper. I was handling both oars by myself while Jesus and Petra carried on about events in her house. I would have loved to ask some questions, but a break did not occur in the conversation, and

The Girl Whose Hand Jesus Touched

I was a little out of breath. I eased up to the dock without a bump, and was the first out of the boat to tie it up.

Jesus looked directly at me when his feet were firmly on the dock. "My blessings I give to you, daughter of Jairus. I know your doubts, but your faith will grow strong when I see you again soon." He was already walking on the rocky shore when I realized I had offered him my hand to help him out of the boat—and he had gratefully accepted. He must be very tired. So, he is human after all. How did he know who I was, and when is he going to see me? Who is this Jesus? I looked at my hand; the calluses from rowing were still there.

DID I DIE?

Several weeks passed. Fishing became much less pleasant when cold water splashed into the boat. The skies had turned grey, and the days grew short. I seldom saw Petra because her father was often gone with Jesus, for he was one of the twelve men who followed Jesus around the countryside. As the oldest child, not only did Petra watch the younger children but she also helped keep up her father's fishing business. The boys of the village went to school to learn Hebrew, but girls did not go to school. In synagogue and in conversations around the village, people discussed the words of Jesus and repeated stories of his activities. Some even started writing down the parables he had spoken. But he stayed away from Capernaum. We heard of the miracles he was doing elsewhere. I wondered about what I had seen. I remembered that he especially told me I would see him again.

Then one morning I woke up with a fever; I did not have strength to get off my cot. Throughout the day and that night, I did not feel better. A doctor came, but the remedies he gave me did not help. I could tell my parents were very concerned. I shivered uncontrollably, and I felt like I was in very cold water. My mother would build up the fire and then sweat ran down my face, which plastered my hair into ringlets on my forehead.

I tried to focus on my father, Jairus, at the foot of my cot, tenderly cradling my feet. His lips moved as though praying. Why are my parents gazing at me so tearfully? I never meant to be such a worry to them. Would I ever be strong enough to go fishing and row my boat again?

Voices became distant. I faintly heard my parents ask each other, "Could anyone heal our precious daughter? What more can we do?"

Scrambling stiffly to his feet, my father leaned near my face and spoke. "We have seen the remarkable miracles of Jesus, right here in Capernaum! He makes cripples walk, people who have been lame from birth. The blind can suddenly see. He does this all with his bare hands and voice alone. I heard he was back in the village today."

My mother eagerly continued the sentence, "Do you think he could possibly come to our daughter and make her well? It is our last hope."

"He did say he would see me again . . . the last time I saw him . . . but he never returned," I remembered. I tried to mouth the words, but they just did not come out.

I heard my father swiftly exit our black stone house. A blast of cold, wintry air chilled me further when he opened the courtyard door. How I wish my mother, now tucking the blanket in closer to my face, did not look so worried!

"Will he remember me?" I faintly murmured. "I was strong then; I could row the boat. I even helped him out of the boat."

"Rest dear, and pray to God for healing," my mother said.

I could no longer muster strength to gather my thoughts as the vision of my mother's weeping face drifted slowly away. Resistance was futile. I was going to another place.

Her father raced through the black stone streets of Capernaum toward the sea where Jesus had last been seen. With his heart about to burst, not only from running, but out of sheer panic, he felt his knees about to buckle. Would he be able to find the young rabbi in time? Could he convince him to rush to his sick daughter's bedside? Swiftly, his eyes sorted through the multitude of people by the water. He was searching for the one person in the world who could possibly help him at this minute. What if his only child was already dead? At this thought, his heart sank; then all hope would be lost. However powerful the healing hands of Jesus may be, was it possible to believe that Jesus could raise the dead to life? Such a miracle was said to have happened once before . . . the son of a widow had been brought back to life in the village of Nain.

Abruptly, he bolted with a new surge of energy. He glimpsed an animated figure whose commanding voice held the multitude in rapt attention. He pushed through the crowd and fell exhausted at Jesus' feet.

"My little daughter lies at the point of death. Come, lay your hands on her that she may be healed and she will live," begged Jairus with his last breath.

The Girl Whose Hand Jesus Touched

Jesus paused in his teaching. He expressed his concern and followed the frantic father who retraced his footsteps back in the direction of his residence. Anticipating some new excitement, the crowd scrambled along as well. But everything was moving in slow motion for Jairus. Why wouldn't the multitude make way for someone as himself who obviously had the greatest need for Jesus now? Still more people were clamoring for Jesus' attention! Precious time passed before they were finally making some progress along the streets. Jairus dared to calm his beating heart. Then, a new commotion broke out. A woman threw herself at Jesus' feet sobbing. Jesus stopped the procession and called her . . . "daughter."

"What about my daughter?" Jairus pleaded. "This woman is at least alive! My daughter may be dead by now!"

Again, the crowd collectively held its breath as each person strained to watch the action. The rumor was that this woman had bled uncontrollably for many years. All possible doctors had failed to help her; now she was out of money with no improvement in her condition. She had just this one last hope. Her faith in Jesus was so strong that she believed if she only touched him her body would be healed. Tentatively she reached for the very fringe of Jesus' robe. A miracle occurred! She felt the healing power surge through her. With great relief she would have gladly slipped back anonymously into the crowd and enjoy her new freedom. That was not to be! Jesus had indeed noticed that healing power had left him and now he demanded, "Who touched me?"

This woman, who was so relieved to be healed, lay mortified on the ground before Jesus. In her enormous faith, she had dared to touch Jesus! She stammered an apology. She had expected to be condemned, but instead soothing words like pure water calmed her heart.

"Daughter, your faith has made you well. Go in peace and your weakness is healed."

For a few seconds Jairus had even forgotten his own terror. But it quickly overwhelmed him again. He anxiously coaxed Jesus in the direction of his house. Now he was convinced. After seeing this miracle, he knew that Jesus could indeed heal his daughter. If only she could hang onto life a few minutes longer!

Scrambling around the corner ahead of him, slipping on loose pebbles, who did he see? His own grim-faced servants came running to meet him, mouthing the words he dreaded to hear: "Your daughter is dead. Why trouble the teacher anymore?"

Bold Girls Speak

His trembling heart failed. Jesus also heard the terrible words, but his answer was curiously calm, "Do not be afraid; only believe, and she will be made well."

What could this possibly mean? Jairus was near collapsing, all hope was drained. Now he was being asked to believe?

Jesus commanded the crowd to stop following him, and they quietly fell back. Only his closest disciples and Jairus approached the residence. Several mourners outside the house door, who raised their voices in horrible wailing, met them.

Jesus said to them, "Why make this commotion and weep? The child is not dead but sleeping." The mourners made little attempt to stifle their ridicule. After all, they were professionals at determining if a person was dead, and this child was dead!

Jairus tried to remember Jesus' words as he entered his house with Jesus and his three closest disciples, Peter, James, and John. His eyes welled up with tears when he viewed the motionless body of his little girl. At her side, his wife was sobbing. Jesus said, "Just sleeping, don't be afraid, only believe."

Then Jesus approached the girl's bedside with a look of love and tenderness in his face. He took her hand and commanded her gently, "*Talitha, cumi.*"

A moment, or perhaps an eternity later, warm breath tickled my ear.

"Talitha, cumi!" The whispered voice was so comforting! Did it come from another world? Had I gone to heaven? Someone firmly held my hand.

The Girl Whose Hand Jesus Touched

"Talitha, cumi." I understood the words perfectly in my native language. The words meant, "Girl, I say to you, get up!"

Suddenly, my legs twitched. I gasped for air, and sat up. Jesus steadied my hand as I struggled to my feet. "Give her something to eat," Jesus commanded. "And don't tell anyone what has happened here today."

"My daughter, is your question answered? Now you know who I am. I have been with you all along, and I will share your boat again," Jesus told me. Then he was gone.

Mother's broth and bread never tasted better. Now I had a new question, "Why shouldn't I tell anyone about this?" Of course, I knew I would tell Petra. After all, her father had been present, and so she would know about this. But I decided not tell anyone else. Well, maybe I needed to tell . . .

POINTS TO PONDER ON THE DAUGHTER OF JAIRUS

How does it feel for this girl to awaken from the dead with her hand in the hand of Jesus? This rabbi, who has attracted so much attention in her village, actually cared enough about her life to come to her bedside. Her fever has lifted. Suddenly, she is strong enough to do her tasks and she can prepare for a future! His concern for her is not over at this point. He even asked that she be given something to eat. She was truly alive, well, and hungry! Her parents were overjoyed. She would never forget this day. Now she celebrates two birthdays. The day she was born and the day she was born again! In a way, all believers are born twice. The first birth is when a baby is born, and the second is when that person knows the saving hand of Jesus. This happens to everyone who believes in Jesus!

On this same very busy day in the life of Jesus, he not only raised this girl from the dead, he also healed a woman who had bled constantly her entire adult life. These two miracles have important things to say, especially to women and girls. Jesus always treated women and children with love and respect. He answered their questions, and they often understood his teaching much better than did the male followers. He never ridiculed women, and he valued their many contributions. He greatly loved many women as true friends, and he made a point to teach them so they could use their full gifts in spreading the good news. The girl in this story is one of many with whom Jesus interacted.

Bold Girls Speak

The stories of this bold girl are included in three Gospels of the New Testament. Read the three versions, Matthew 9:18–25; Mark 5:21–43; Luke 8:40–56, and note the minor variations. As in all ten of these *Bold Girls* stories, be sure to note the parts that are fictional and the parts that are from the Bible. This girl is unnamed in the three Gospel accounts, so she remains unnamed in this *Bold Girl* story. I added a friend, Petra, who is the fictional daughter of Peter. Given that Peter had a mother-in-law, which is known from the healing miracle at Peter's house that was illustrated in this *Bold Girls* account, we know that Peter was married. He could have had a family, and traditions have survived about his wife who accompanied him to Rome. According to an early legend, Peter had a daughter named Petronilla who was a first-century martyr. A woman named Petronilla did actually live, but it is uncertain that she was a daughter of Peter. Petra's part in this story is totally made up, but a "best friend" adds another person with whom the main character can interact. Look up the names and stories of people who lost their lives because of their belief in Jesus as the Son of God.

This is also the only *Bold Girls* story where the main character girl does not use her voice according to the biblical text. Although the conversations in this *Bold Girls* story are totally fictional, they contain the reactions and questions that young people might have had as eyewitnesses to the early ministry of Jesus. The bold girl of this story struggles with the identity of Jesus who appears to be both human and also divine. People at that time, and today, struggle with the same question. Discuss this with your class and teachers.

The first six chapters of Mark were used to write this *Bold Girls* story. These chapters of Mark are packed with the early events of Jesus' ministry. There are many subjects to discuss: the nature and purpose of the miracles; parables; choosing the disciples; rejection in his hometown; relations with his biological family; and the people opposing Jesus. In these chapters of Mark, Jesus confronts demons and unclean spirits. What do you make of these?

The daughter of Jairus is not heard from again in the New Testament. But no doubt this girl will learn much more about Jesus and the biggest miracle of all that he performs for those who believe in him. In this *Bold Girls* story, that miracle will occur a few years in the future, which is when Jesus died on the cross and arose again to forgive our sins. It is easy to imagine that this bold girl quickly started telling everyone she knew about the miracle she herself experienced, as other recipients of Jesus' miracles told tales of their own experiences. It is also easy to imagine that for the rest of her life she told of this amazing wonder she experienced over and over, to her children and grandchildren and anyone else who would listen. Why is this girl's name not mentioned? Certainly, Jesus wrote it in the Book of Life.

QUESTIONS FOR DISCUSSION

1. The following passages tell us about Jesus raising someone from the dead. Were these people all great and important people?
   - Luke 7:11–17: The unnamed son of the widow of Nain.
   - Luke 8:40–56: The unnamed daughter of Jairus.
   - John 11:1–44: Lazarus, the brother of Mary and Martha in Bethany.
2. Why did Jesus perform miracles? Did he heal people to make people happy and love him, or to show who he is? How do the miracles show who Jesus is?
3. Why doesn't Jesus raise all people from the dead? Why did he allow these people to die in the first place before he raised them from the dead?
4. Why does Jesus tell those who benefit from his miracles not to tell anyone?
5. When will all people on earth be raised from the dead?
6. How can Jesus have the power to heal people from diseases and bring them to life again?
7. Does Jesus still heal people today?
8. Did the father's faith save the girl? If a person has enough faith, why can't all of his or her loved ones be healed and saved from death?

RELATED TOPICS TO EXPLORE

1. The family of Jairus is one of the few families mentioned in the New Testament with a father, mother, and children. It was wonderful that this bold girl had two parents to care for her when she was sick, but do all children have this advantage?
2. On what other occasions does Jesus pay special attention to children?

3. What can you do now and in the future to help women and girls in many lands who do not have the same privileges as the men and boys?

4. Jesus spent much time crossing the Sea of Galilee in boats. Look up the "Jesus Boat" that was found on the shore of the lake in 1986. It is a first-century boat that may be like the ones used at the time of this story. Have boats changed much over two millennia?

5. The village of Capernaum can be seen today, as can many nearby sites associated with Jesus. Look at maps and find photos of these areas as tourists see it today.

6. Jesus seemed to be distant from the main character of this *Bold Girls* story for a while. But by the end of this story, this bold girl realizes that Jesus was with her all the time, even before she knew who he was. Have you had times when you thought Jesus was absent, but you later understood how he was with you all along?

SUGGESTED TOPICS OF DISCUSSION FOR TEACHERS AND PARENTS OF OLDER STUDENTS

1. Are baby daughters always accepted into the family with as much joy as baby sons?

    What are the differences in medical care and educational opportunities that boys and girls receive in some parts of the world?

2. Many commentaries note that women were separated from the men in the synagogue, but in the ruins of the few first-century synagogues still in existence, no evidence of this custom has been found in the form of balconies, stairs, or barriers. The synagogue ruins that can be seen in Capernaum today date from the fourth century. The exact customs of the first century are unknown. Do you think it is a distraction for men and women, girls and boys to worship together in church or should they sit in separate sections? Should girls and boys go to school together and sit in the same classes or do they learn better separated? Some religions teach that men and women should not have contact with each other, unless they are relatives. What are the pros and cons of this way of life?

3. This story offers an opportunity to discuss menstruation and the many ways that attitudes toward women's bodies have changed over

the centuries. What are problems that women face in less privileged parts of the world concerning personal hygiene? In some countries, during this time of the month women are isolated in a filthy hut and girls are prevented from going to school. How do women manage without the convenient disposable products that are available today?

4. Mark 5:25–34 is the story of the woman with a flow of blood. Refer to Leviticus 12:7 concerning both normal and abnormal discharges of both men and women. How should we understand the Old Testament passages about uncleanliness? How do they apply today or why do these laws not apply today? Nothing in this passage actually concerns her being ceremonially unclean. This is an important point to consider, and the conclusions you draw may be contrary to many existing commentaries. If touching a dead girl or a woman who is bleeding would make Jesus ceremonially impure, it does not seem to be an important issue to Mark. It is important to remember that Mark is communicating to a Gentile audience in his Gospel, and he would have made a clarification of Jewish customs if it were crucial to understanding the events he describes here. The important point is that the woman was unwell and then she was healed.

The Maids Who Questioned
Matthew 26:69–75; Mark 14:66–72; Luke 22:54–62; John 18:15–27

A STRANGE MAN KNOCKS AT THE BACK DOOR

"In the hectic time of Passover preparations, why am I being summoned upstairs by one of Caiaphas's accountants?" asked Abby, a kitchen maid. It was still morning and already she was frazzled. "I never go into that section of the palace; did we spend too much on the food budget?" she asked Liz, another cook.

"Go on, I'll take over here," Liz offered. "I hope it will be quick; we certainly can't return the ingredients that we already put into the charoseth," she sniffed. "Must the head steward always be so persnickety about every nut and raisin? There is no lack of funds for everything else."

Abby scampered up the marble stairs and hurried through frescoed hallways until she reached the accountants. Of course, she would not see the chief priest, Caiaphas, as he was already at the Temple for Passover sacrifices. Apparently, the steward was expecting her; she found him waiting in his office. Her concern about being pulled away from the busy kitchen for no good reason was unwarranted.

"Take this bag down with you to the kitchen. A man will be coming by the servant's entrance in the back courtyard to pick this up," was all that he told Abby.

"What do you mean? Shouldn't I know more?" The bag felt heavy with the weight of many coins.

The Maids Who Questioned

"That's all I know," the accountant told her. "Oh, his name is Judas, and he will speak with a Galilean accent. We servants up here don't get told any more than you do, down in the kitchen."

Abby retraced her steps back down to the kitchen carrying the weight of the bag, the weight of responsibility, and some foreboding. If someone questioned her about this bag, she could be accused of stealing. Hopefully, the situation would soon become more obvious. Perhaps it was payment to some Galilean merchant for produce.

"Good, that didn't take too long," Liz was buried up to her elbows in greens. "What was that about?"

"I am not sure. Did we get a delivery of wine from Galilee?" Abby asked. "I have a bag of coins I am supposed to give to a Galilean man who will arrive at the servant's door."

"That would explain it; we do have several new amphora of Galilean wine," Liz noted. "There is so much going on today it will be easy to miss someone expecting payment," she continued. "Put the bag somewhere safe, and we will keep an eye on the courtyard."

According to tradition, the preparations for Passover were to be completed by midday, although the servants could finish tasks that had already been started. Practically, as Abby complained to Liz, that meant the servants would be cooking all afternoon, serving at dusk, and cleaning up well into the night. Of course, the family of Caiaphas would enjoy the results of all the preparations, hardly aware of the extra work necessary to present such a feast at Passover. At dusk, the family would come to the table with guests and enjoy the savory efforts of many unseen hands.

Abby kept an eye on the servant's courtyard all morning. A very healthy lamb was tied to a post and bleated pathetically. Abby slipped it some water and feed, a rather futile attempt to offer it some comfort. This animal was the special, unblemished lamb that would be taken by one of the head male servants to the Temple this afternoon. The cold cellar held more freshly butchered lambs, because many would be needed for the feast tonight. Even the servants would get a fresh lamb for their much more modest Passover celebration in the kitchen. This particular animal, still very much alive, would be sacrificed at the Jerusalem Temple as a sort of representative of the rest of the lambs.

At midday, an insistent knock at the back door reminded Abby of the bag of money she had secured. She peaked through a window with some trepidation. If she made a mistake, the consequences for her would be severe. "What if I gave the bag to the wrong person?" she whispered to Liz on her way to the door.

"I am expected at this entrance," the man plainly stated.

"Um . . . what is your name?" Abby asked.

"Judas, I am here for the thirty pieces of silver," Abby detected the Galilean accent.

"Wait here," she left to retrieve the bag. "Thirty pieces of silver," she thought to herself. "That is not much for all this wine. Well, we servants don't ask questions, just obey."

"Here you are sir, enjoy your Passover," Abby added. She presented the heavy bag to the man. He did not return greetings, and his stony face did not crack a smile in return as he took the bag from her.

"I hope the wine is not sour," she told Liz upon returning. "He is not in a very festive mood. That guy seemed relieved he was actually going to be paid, as though the house of Caiaphas cannot pay its bills."

A PASSOVER SACRIFICE TO REMEMBER

Joe and Simon, both stable keepers, came into the kitchen. "There is no one available to take the lamb to the Temple this afternoon," Simon said while looking for a morsel to eat. "They seem to be very busy with something else upstairs. We got word from above that one of us needs to represent the house of Caiaphas at the sacrifice."

Liz gave a bit of food to Simon. "Here is the last piece of bread. We must have all the yeast out of the kitchen before tonight," she added. During Passover, the Jews could eat only unleavened bread in memory of the Exodus when the Israelites escaped from Egypt. "The children will be coming through the kitchen tonight to search for any scrap of yeast."

"Well, has either one of you ever seen the Passover at the Temple?" Abby asked hesitantly.

"I have only seen it from the Court of the Women with my mother many years ago. Every household in Jerusalem has to bring a lamb to be sacrificed. I remember a multitude of lambs and men crammed into a small place," said Joe.

"How do they manage that number of sacrifices?" Abby asked. "Every year we are always busy with preparations and cannot attend. You know that this is the one sacrifice where the priest does not kill the animal but the offerer bringing the sheep."

"That is a lot of bleating sheep, blood and guts, and sweaty men, I can imagine," said Liz.

"Yes, one does watch where you put your feet," said Simon. "Where there are animals, it is . . . slippery."

"Well, which one of you is going to slit the throat of that lovely young sheep out there in the courtyard?" Abby asked.

"We do have to put a horse down once in a while," Simon offered thoughtfully. "If one gets injured or too old, we take it to the dump outside the walls and . . ."

"Never mind!" Abby interrupted. "I have heard enough! So who is going?" Simon and Joe looked at each other.

"We will cast lots," suggested Liz. "What could we use?" she glanced around the kitchen. "Close your eyes. I will have a nut in one hand. The one who chooses the hand with the nut goes." Liz picked up an almond and hid it in one of her hands behind her back.

Abby noted that Joe looked a little pale when he came up the "winner." She quickly asked, "Can I go with you?"

"Of course," Joe seemed hesitant. "But you know that women can't go into the Court of the Israelites where the sacrifices take place."

"Sure, I know that," Abby was a little surprised that he called her a woman. "But I can watch from above on the wall that separates the Court of the Women from the altar area. I've heard the view is good enough to absorb the atmosphere, but not too close to see everything that I really don't want to see."

"Thanks for coming with me; we will leave soon to get into the first round of sacrifices," Joe seemed relieved.

From the palace of Caiaphas, Joe and Abby slowly made their way to the Temple. The streets were crowded. For Passover, people came from all over Judea, Galilee, and from the far reaches of the Roman Empire. Joe and Abby, normally confined to the palace by their duties, had never before experienced the confusion of languages and humanity that the celebration brought to Jerusalem. They made faster progress when they entered the bridge over the Tyropoeon Valley, which funneled the crowd directly into the courtyards of the Temple Mount.

The scene was more chaotic than they had expected. People were pushing forward into the Court of the Women with their bleating sheep in tow. No matter how often she had seen it, Abby always gasped at the sight of the Temple facade that towered above. At the fifteen rounded stairs before

Nicanor's Gate, they parted ways. Joe with the sheep, continued into the Court of the Israelites. Abby turned right to enter a long, narrow building with a flat roof, which formed the barrier between the Court of the Women and the Court of the Israelites. She climbed the stairs to get to the roof and there she joined the other women who were eager to observe.

The crowd grew quiet when trumpets began to blast, and the choir of the Levites sang the first notes. Even the sheep seemed aware of Passover's solemnity; they appeared stunned by the unfamiliar environment. Some were being carried to their deaths on the shoulders of their offerer; others were forced to stand on their hind legs for lack of space. Abby strained to find Joe. She saw that he had placed the sheep between his legs to keep it under control. "Is there a special heaven for Passover sheep?" she wondered.

The men had their knives ready, and the priests faced them, each with a bowl to catch the blood. Then it started; the row of sheep facing the priests slumped to the floor when their throats were slit. The gushing blood spilled into silver and golden bowls, which flashed in the light as they were quickly exchanged back and forth to more priests standing at the altar. They splashed the blood against the base of the altar, and the slaughtered sheep were split down the belly to remove the entrails. The priests expertly cut the fat away, which was placed on the altar fire.

Soon smoke was rising high into the sky and the smell of burning fat assaulted Abby's nose. The priests removed the skin and hung the animal carcasses on hooks. All the cutting and butchering was synchronized as a sort of a dance by priests who had done it many times. Abby could not catch Joe's performance as a first-time offerer, but she hoped he noted which sheep belonged to the house of Caiaphas. When the last echoes of the Hallel faded away, the men collected their now cleaned sheep and headed out the side doors. A quick mop-up followed the retreating men before a new crowd entered. This went on for at least three cycles, until every household in Jerusalem had sacrificed a sheep. Abby and Joe managed to find each other at the exits. The sheep's feet were tied together and it was hanging from a stick, which Joe carried over his shoulder. Soon it would be roasting on a spit over a fire in the servant's courtyard.

"So, what did you think of the Passover sacrifice," Abby faced Joe who looked pale and blood splattered.

"It is the celebration of God's goodness toward Israel and his deliverance of Israel out of Egypt," Joe gave the practiced answer.

"Well, yes I know that," Abby was rather indignant. "But, what did you really think of the whole experience as a participant?"

"Could you see my hands shaking from your place on the wall?" Joe admitted. "I made sure my knife was very sharp and just did what the other men did. I hope they didn't notice what an amateur I am."

"I saw Caiaphas standing well back from the whole mess. Blood could not be splashed on his priceless robes," said Abby. "Anyway, current events have distracted him lately with all the Roman soldiers in the city."

"Yes, the tension is palpable," Joe continued. "Jesus of Nazareth is causing serious discussion about very necessary changes, and the leaders, like our master, as the chief priest, have the most to lose."

THE SERVANTS ASK

"This Jesus of Nazareth, is he really the promised Messiah, the son of David?" Abby hesitantly tossed the question out to her fellow servants while sorting bitter herbs. Shadows had already lengthened inside the servant's courtyard, and they watched the lambs roasting on the fire.

"No way; he is a rabble rouser. He preaches insurrection!" Liz paused in her sweeping and punctuated her speech by jabbing the broom into the pavement stones. "Master Caiaphas says that if Jesus is allowed to continue teaching in the temple, a riot cannot be stopped. Roman soldiers will move in, and there will be plenty of trouble."

"I agree," answered Simon. "I saw him in the Temple the other day when he shoved over the merchants' tables. Coins rolled into the pavement cracks and caged doves flew free when their cages sprang open. Tempers flared and shouting echoed between the walls. Feathers and money flew everywhere. Who does he think he is to disturb the peace in this way?"

"Yes, on that day Caiaphas came home looking mighty irritated; his long beard must have been really itchy," added Liz. "Our master is the chief priest of the Sanhedrin, and he is ultimately responsible to maintain order in the Temple. Now, with crowds of country people coming into Jerusalem for Passover, they have to maintain the peace. Those backward people from Galilee are so easily agitated."

"Jesus is not a violent man at all," said Joe. He put down his basket of charcoal. "I saw him entering Jerusalem on the Sabbath, riding a donkey. The crowds were cheering him with songs, 'Hosanna to the Son of David!

Blessed be he that cometh in the name of the Lord.' They were waving palms and laying coats on his path."

As the work of Passover was winding down, the servants could pause for their own modest Passover celebration. The servers were already upstairs in the dining room for the banquet of Caiaphas and his guests. Now that Abby, Liz, and the others had finished the preparations they had time to continue the same arguments heard all over the city during this week of Passover. Everyone, from the highest officials of the synagogue to the merchants in the market, was discussing the man from Nazareth, Jesus. Could he be the long awaited King, the Messiah of the Jews, or was he, like so many others, a fraud? Joe and Abby were convinced that Jesus was truly the Messiah and was treated unjustly. Liz and Simon thought Jesus was a troublemaker. They were all worried about the unsettled times and what the future held for them, as well as for Jerusalem.

With a loud crack, snapped tree branches showered dried olive leaves on the small group. Riotous squawking and a burst of feathers brought the conversation to a stop when a flustered chicken fell to the ground in front of them.

"That old rooster again, why don't we catch him for our own Sabbath dinner?" Liz said to Simon who halfheartedly tried to grab the bird as it escaped. "It must have come over the city wall from the poorer housing below. Caiaphas would be furious at such a lowly intruder."

"That bird is even tougher than you!" Simon teased her. "You would have to boil him over the fire for a whole week before he would be tender enough to eat."

The Maids Who Questioned

"Well then, I hope his crowing outside your loft keeps waking you up nights. He seems to be attracted to men who talk too much!" Liz answered him back.

Abby interrupted the horseplay. "The palace is full of guests, and the front gate guards report that more are still arriving. Why would the whole Sanhedrin be coming here on Passover eve? Surely, they would rather celebrate with their own families. They seem preoccupied, not in the mood for any celebration."

"It has to do with that fellow, Jesus," said Aaron, one of the stable keepers who had joined the group. "I spied Pontius Pilate approaching the citadel this morning with a legion of Roman soldiers. You can be sure that when the governor comes to Jerusalem, something is going on. The rumor has it that a trial is being set."

"What can they try him for?" Abby asked. "Jesus has healed people who are lame, and has driven away evil spirits. The whole city is exclaiming how he raised Lazarus from the grave. He teaches forgiveness and love even for the enemy. I would like to learn more about him."

"Don't forget, he heals on the Sabbath," Liz said, raising her voice, "which is clearly breaking the law. What will he try next? He has been responsible for one absurd event after the other!"

Insistent knocking at the back gate interrupted the argument. "Who wants in now? Even a palace can't hold many more people," said Simon. Abby wondered what sort of strange character could be at the back gate. At this time, people should be at home celebrating with their families.

"I hope it is the owner of that rooster. I'm tired of cleaning up the droppings under its roosting limb," said Liz.

"We do have to be careful about who is coming in the back gate. For good reason, the house of Caiaphas is known as a place of intrigue and whisperings," said Aaron who got around outside the palace more than the others. "Tonight more so than ever."

"I also saw Jesus last Sabbath when he came through the Damascus gate riding on a donkey," Abby remembered. "He looked like a man of many sorrows. He would be handsome if he didn't seem to be carrying the weight of the world on his shoulders."

"You were speaking of a handsome man?" asked Liz, suddenly paying attention.

"You have only one thing on your mind, Liz," Abby chided. "Honestly, some beauty is more than skin deep. I was thinking of Jesus. What I have heard about him is very convincing. What if he is the promised Messiah our Jewish nation has longed for since the days of Isaiah the prophet?"

"Messiah or not, I have been eavesdropping under the window and overhearing arguments going on all evening in the upper chamber. I have never seen the household so tense," said Aaron, who was just off front gate duty. "The night is going to be very long, and we will have to keep the fire going."

The double back gates, normally used for deliveries by wagons and horses, were flung open by guards in full armor. They took no notice of the servants. Numerous torches held high against the night sky suddenly illuminated the courtyard. The servants' Passover feast and conversation came to an abrupt end.

"They didn't even announce themselves!" Abby said with indignation. "How do we know who has entered?"

"They are Temple guards under the control of Caiaphas; I know some of them," said Aaron after he recovered from the surprise. "They don't need to act like they own the place."

Then the servants all fell silent, horrified at the sight unfolding before their eyes. These guards dragged, more than escorted, one badly bruised man across the courtyard toward the palace.

"Isn't that the Jesus of Nazareth you were speaking of?" Liz whispered to Abby.

"It can't be . . . but it seems to be. How horrible! How can they be so cruel to someone who has been kind to so many?" Abby gasped.

A DAY NEVER FORGOTTEN

The horrified household servants formed a tight group as they watched the brutal parade disappear into the back door of the palace. Immediately, the windows upstairs lit up from all the torches being carried inside. The palace almost looked like it was on fire. The shouting slowly subsided and the voice of Caiaphas echoed from the interior, his speech not quite distinguishable.

Uneasiness gripped the shivering servants as the guards returned into the courtyard. But instead of departing, the guards settled around the fire and made all indications that they would be staying awhile. The servants could not resist slyly edging over to within earshot of the animated conversation among them.

The Maids Who Questioned

"What a night!" one of the guards shouted. His voice carried across the courtyard. "I had my ear sliced off and now it is healed back on better than before. This is unbelievable! Do my ears match?" One guard pretended concern for his appearance and looked at another for an opinion.

"Can you believe the audacious behavior of that disciple of his?" Another boisterous voice rose over the crackling fire. "This guy, Peter I think is his name, went and sliced your ear off... whack... with this huge sword. Like he was going to be some big hero or something... did he think that he would scare us away?" The guards all slapped their thighs and roared with laughter.

"Oh yeah, I was shaking in my sandals... like this," another guard said. He stood to make a mocking imitation with his knees knocking together.

"Hey, that is Malchus," Aaron elbowed Simon excitedly. "He's a personal guard of Caiaphas. His ear looks fine to me; they just like to brag." Their attentions were quickly drawn back to the conversation of the guards. "Healed me, just like that," Malchus snapped his fingers.

"So, who is this motley soul, Jesus, we arrested tonight? Some kind of healer! Sure to be a magic trick," another guard joined in.

"No, it is for real; I saw it, too! This Jesus guy, he just touched your ear and it was reattached. It was a miracle," a guard said to Malchus. "What is going on up there in the palace?"

"I imagine he is under arrest. His own followers are trying to help him, and he goes and heals the enemy. Like, whose side is he on, man?" another guard asked.

"'For all who take the sword will perish by the sword.' Those are his exact words," a guard who had been silent, so far, quoted in a thoughtful voice.

The servants huddled just within earshot; they glanced around at each other, scarcely believing their ears.

Liz noticed a solitary man off to the side who looked a little nervous. She looked again, clearly puzzled.

"Hey Abby, did you let that guy in?" Liz whispered. "Who is he? Did he slip in with the guards?"

"He must have been following the crowd," Abby admitted. "Do we need to check him out?"

"You are too trusting. Now go find out for sure." Liz pushed her in his direction. "We need to know who is in here or we could be in big trouble."

Bold Girls Speak

"Does it have to be me?" Abby asked, resigned. "Well, if he is one of the followers of Jesus, maybe I can find out something."

The others watched out of a corner of their eyes as Abby approached the withdrawn figure.

"Sir, I need to ask. You are not also one of this man's disciples, are you?"

"I do not know or understand what you are talking about," the man answered with a gruff voice.

Abby was taken aback by the ferociousness of the man's answer. He exited the yard with unusual haste.

"Hey, that rooster is back and crowing in the middle of the night," Aaron exclaimed. "Of course with all the light and activity around here tonight, the dumb bird probably thinks it is daytime." His attempt at comic relief fell flat.

They kept the fire roaring. The guards continued the animated discussion. The empty bravado would cease every time the roar of sixty or so men in the upstairs room of the palace blasted through the night air.

"Whatever could be going on?" fretted Abby. "I do hope they at least give that man Jesus a fair chance."

"Oh, I fear that Caiaphas, his father-in-law Annas, and the other big beards, have their minds already made up about Jesus," Joe added doubtfully.

"I heard Caiaphas pronounce, 'Better to have one person die for the people, than have many perish,'" said Simon. "Riots will certainly break out if something isn't done quickly."

"But Jesus is not the one getting the people all riled up. If the authorities would just really listen to him, they would understand. He is talking about a different kingdom, an eternal kingdom, not the Roman Empire. I am convinced he is an innocent man," said Abby.

"Hey, there's that guy again," Aaron noted ominously. "Someone else approach him. I don't think he is up to any good. Liz, your turn . . . see what you can find out."

"No way, he seems to be in a foul mood. Come with me," Liz urged. "All right, I'll just shout from here." She turned toward the dejected figure. "Hey you, surely you are with Jesus. You talk like a Galilean."

"I swear I do not know what you are talking about!" roared the man. He let loose a string of profanities and abruptly turned away.

The Maids Who Questioned

"Whoa! He is elevating his conviction with an oath," Simon said under his breath. "That is usually a sure sign of a lie." The rooster, now sounding rather irritated, let out a screech at the disturbance.

"It does seem like something is weighing heavily on his conscience," Abby remarked. "He is a troubled man. No doubt he is very concerned about Jesus."

Shouting voices from the window above got the attention of the courtyard inhabitants. "You have heard his blasphemy!" a voice thundered.

"That is Caiaphas! I know it is him!" said Joe in despair. His voice was then drowned out by cries from above, "Death to him! Death to Jesus!"

The little group of servants stood transfixed by the proceedings, eyes glued to the windows above.

Abby fought back sobs and started whispering a prayer.

Aaron shrugged his shoulders and tried to warm his arms.

Liz sighed and stared blankly straight ahead.

Simon looked down and shuffled his feet in the dust.

Joe felt a lump form in his throat and he clinched his fist. He stole a glance over at the Galilean man sitting on a bench by himself. Abby caught Joe's eye and nodded.

Joe cautiously approached the man, "Certainly you are one of them; your way of speaking makes it obvious."

"I do not know the man!" he growled back with accented expletives. He stood up with such violence that the heavy wooden bench fell backward on the stone pavement with a loud crack.

For the third time, the night air was pierced with the shriek of a rooster. Even the stones seemed to rattle at the sound.

The heavy double doors from the palace flung open into the service courtyard and crashed against the walls. Out poured a crowd of priests in disheveled robes. Snapping to attention, the guards grabbed their gear, which was strewn around the dying fire. The household servants retreated into the shadows for their own safety. Priests and guards shoved each other through the courtyard, making their way to the gate with gruesome purpose. With his hands bound, held upright between two guards, the man Jesus could barely walk. It was obvious to the servants that he had been severely beaten. Jesus staggered through the courtyard, passing the servants closely. His face briefly showed recognition of the Galilean man who did not return any emotion.

"He has the weight of the world on his shoulders," Abby said in despair. "There is something more going on here . . . if I weren't so helpless . . . Oh, Yahweh help Jesus!"

Several guards scrambled behind the receding mob, determined to carry out what could only be a deadly mission. The mob exited the courtyard, leaving the gates standing ajar. The Galilean man stumbled out of the courtyard, barely staying on his feet. Soon the loudest sound was that of insane sobs echoing over from the other side of the wall.

"That man is beyond all help," Liz finally murmured.

Rays of rosy light began to brighten the eastern sky. Silence slowly returned to the courtyard as the noise of the crowd moved away in the direction of the citadel. A new day would soon dawn, bringing with it a new round of chores. But then the servants remembered it was Passover. They retreated to their lofts to catch a few winks of sleep because of the holiday. In the olive tree above, the rooster had finally found peace and was soundly roosting with his head tucked under his wing.

Abby felt the warmth of an arm lay across her shoulder. "Tonight will be a night not soon forgotten," whispered Joe, who had paused beside her. "What will this day bring?"

"Nothing will be the same again. Something has changed," Abby replied. She felt the ground tremble slightly.

POINTS TO PONDER ABOUT THE MAIDS OF CAIAPHAS

This is an imaginative account of what might have gone on between the servants in the courtyard of Caiaphas the night before the crucifixion of Jesus. What can be learned from the conversations of the servant girls and the male servants who appear in this scene? Why do some of the servants seek to know Jesus and others dismiss him? Why does the message of Jesus often fall on fertile ground and other times it falls among the rocks?

This is a story so familiar, yet maybe it is not. Have you ever considered these events from the perspective of the servants? The story of Jesus' trial and crucifixion is recorded in all four of the New Testament Gospels.

The Maids Who Questioned

Between the accounts of Matthew, Mark, Luke, and John, variations occur; but in each of the accounts, Peter's denials were made in answer to questioning by either the same or two different servant girls, and also perhaps by a male servant at the house of Caiaphas. Why are servant girls, of all people, especially mentioned with Peter's denial and the trial of Jesus?

"You will all fail me this night" (Mark 14:30–31), Jesus told his disciples earlier on that evening, after they had eaten Passover together.

"Even though all the others may fail you, I will never leave you, even if I must die with you," Peter reassured Jesus.

"Before the rooster crows twice, you will deny three times that you even know me," Jesus rebuked him.

Please note that the first section of this *Bold Girls* story about the main character's encounter with Judas is fictional. Can you imagine how the betrayal of Judas was set up? This is only one possible scenario, and your version of events may be better. The scene of the Passover sacrifices in the Temple is told with as much detail as can be reconstructed from descriptions from the first century. The details of how Passover was prepared in the grand palace of Caiaphas, from the point of view of the maids, are also imaginary. The conversations and the issues being discussed between the servants reveal the tensions and doubts of common people, which Jesus had raised by his actions of the previous days.

Be sure to read and compare the accounts of Jesus' trial that is found in all four Gospels (Matt 26–27; Mark 15; Luke 22–23; John 18–19). When the servants notice Peter, he becomes their main attraction in the courtyard. Remember, the servants can only speculate about the details of the trial that is going on in the grand rooms of the palace. The servants' questioning of Peter is sort of a parallel trial going on at the same time as the trial of Jesus in the marble halls of the high priest. Could Peter not have supported Jesus as a true witness in Jesus' defense? Instead he stayed by a fire in the courtyard to warm himself.

Young women play an important part in this episode of Peter's denial of Christ. As in all the *Bold Girls* stories, these girls used their voices, asserted themselves, and solved problems on their own. In many ways, servant girls had more freedoms than the daughters of the master of the house. Upper class daughters would have been closely guarded so their future marriage prospects would not be tarnished. Servants, in contrast, had freedom to run errands all over the city. They had contact with many different kinds of people, and they probably became quite perceptive in the ways of the world. From ancient writings, it is recorded that the house of Caiaphas had a reputation as a house of whisperings and intrigue. We are reminded again, as in the other *Bold Girls* stories, that it is not always the high and mighty who know the truth of what is really going on. These girls no doubt knew how to use their ears and voices, and did so on the night of Peter's betrayal.

The servants, particularly the servant girls, controlled the action in the courtyard. Maybe they were naive enough to approach someone unknown, while mature bystanders may have been afraid to ask for the truth. These young servants did not have such pretensions. A lesson that could be learned here is that Peter's words to servant girls should have been as truthful and earnestly answered as the words given to important authorities. A person is accountable for all words he or she speaks or hears, no matter the rank and importance of the speaker or listener. God does not respect people because of their earthly standing. Jesus said the high must become low and the low high. That evening, Peter should have sat down with the servants and talked to them of Jesus! After all, Jesus himself took time to talk to women and children.

Peter is one of Jesus' closest disciples and is an important character in three of our *Bold Girls* stories. Peter is an interesting disciple to study closely; he wrote two short books of the New Testament. If you are reading these stories in chronological order, then you have already met Peter in the story of the daughter of Jairus. That story occurred early in the ministry of Jesus. This story of the servants of Caiaphas is at the end of Jesus' life. We next meet Peter during Rhoda's story, which occurs about ten or more years later. Be sure to note that fifty days after the crucifixion, Peter will quote the words of the Old Testament prophet, Joel, on Pentecost: "Even on my slaves, both men and women, I will pour forth of my Spirit in those last days and they will prophesy." Peter would be a strong leader again on the day when flames appeared on the heads of the gathering of early Christians. However, on this night when Peter denied knowing Jesus, his faith wavered. He experienced weakness and, no doubt, great fear. How many people in the Bible, and also in history, have displayed great strength, as well as great weakness?

Were these maids of Caiaphas believers in Jesus and part of the newfound faith? Or did these maids adhere to the position of their master, Caiaphas? Either possibility can be imagined, which is why in this *Bold Girls* scenario one girl believes in Jesus and the other girl is skeptical.

Considering their outgoing personalities and willingness to confront Peter, it would be impossible to imagine that these girls were totally indifferent or ignorant of the happenings in Jerusalem at that time.

All four of the Gospel writers remember the roles the servant girls play in the overall crucifixion story. However, these servant girls are neither honored nor sainted, and no songs or poems are written about them. These girls are nonetheless present for generations of believers to ponder, and this *Bold Girls* story provides a possible glimpse into an important moment in their lives. They lived their humble lives as servant girls in the household of Caiaphas in Jerusalem at the time of the trial of Jesus, but they were also eyewitnesses to an important part of the event. They took their jobs seriously and knew what was going on in the courtyard. They spoke up, they pointed out the truth of the situation, and they had the courage to speak out.

Were they at all changed by participating in this momentous event? What did they think when darkness fell over the city of Jerusalem the next day? How did they react when the news of the crucifixion reached them the next day? We will never know to whom they recounted the story in the coming weeks and years, but Christ-followers increased dramatically in the early years, which means that the message spread. Even in our smallest jobs, we may never know what impact our actions and words will have on others. God works through the small as well as the mighty. That could be the lesson of these servant girls.

QUESTIONS FOR DISCUSSION

1. Review the events of Jesus' life that led up to the crucifixion as they are told in all four Gospels (Matt 26–27; Mark 15; Luke 22–23; John 18–19). Compare the details of events between the four Gospels. How do they differ?
2. What was the meaning of Passover, and what preparations would be necessary to celebrate it?
3. What other women observed important events of the crucifixion of Jesus?
4. Who were the Sanhedrin, the Sadducees, and the Pharisees?
5. Was Peter on trial in the courtyard at the same time Jesus was on trial inside the palace? How were their trials the same and different?

Bold Girls Speak

6. What were the issues that the Sanhedrin accused Jesus of at the trial? What were their arguments against Jesus? Why did they hate him?

7. Why did Peter deny Christ, outside of the fact that Jesus said it would happen? What was he afraid of? Peter and all the disciples were no doubt very afraid that they would also be arrested. Perhaps Peter was afraid he would be called in to the trial in the house of Caiaphas to be a witness.

RELATED CULTURAL AND HISTORICAL QUESTIONS TO EXPLORE

1. How did the lives of girls at that time differ according to the class in which they were born? For instance, compare how the daughters of Caiaphas lived in luxury while the lives of the servant girls were filled with hard work. The servant girls may have actually been slaves, yet they probably lived better than many other children.

2. What was the relationship of Judea to the Roman Empire at this time? Who were the rulers?

3. Why were animal sacrifices such a common part of ancient worship in many cultures? Look up Leviticus 17 to find out why blood was carefully drained away. Why are animal sacrifices no longer a part of our worship?

4. Are you interested in a career in law? What elements of the trial of Jesus still exist in a trial today? What were the many reasons his trial was not valid at that time?

5. Some of the servants of Caiaphas probably became Christ-followers. How did the lives of believers in Christ and the rest of the Jews diverge in the near future? What is their relationship today?

SUGGESTED TOPICS OF DISCUSSION FOR TEACHERS AND PARENTS OF OLDER STUDENTS

1. The meaning and importance of animal sacrifice is difficult to understand, and it is very strange in modern culture. What is the Old Testament history and origin of animal sacrifice? What was the prevalence

The Maids Who Questioned

of sacrifice in parallel cultures? Are there modern equivalents of sacrifices? How are the animals that we consume for food killed? Read the rules laid down in the Old Testament to discover ways to take care that an animal is killed in a humane manner.

2. As her fictional role is told in this *Bold Girls* story, was Abby an unknowing accessory to a crime? What circumstances can you imagine that could create this situation, both ancient and modern? What is the degree of guilt carried by a person who inadvertently helps a criminal commit a crime?

3. In Luke 22:3 we read: "Satan entered Judas." What is the origin of evil? Why was Judas the betrayer of Jesus and not another disciple? How is Judas responsible for the betrayal of Jesus if Satan caused it?

4. In the Garden of Gethsemane when the disciples repeatedly fall asleep, Jesus warns them to pray that they "do not fall into temptation" (Mark 14:38). Why is it so important for us to constantly pray that we do not fall into temptation?

5. Why and in how many ways are women restricted from full participation in the activities of the Jewish Temple and synagogue? Likewise, in the Christian church, how are women restricted? Are these restrictions a correct interpretation of scripture?

Rhoda, the Servant Girl Who Persisted

ACTS 12:5–17

ESCAPE

WITH HER LAST GASP of breath, a desperate girl stumbled across the threshold to safety. Once she was inside Daphne's Grove, no one could capture her. She felt for the lumps in her bag. Only a few minutes ago she had stolen a few apricots at the market of Antioch. The quick search of the bag reassured her that all were accounted for, and she was so hungry. Normally she was much cleverer at snatching her food. Today, however, a couple of foreign-looking men had witnessed her commit the crime. They halfheartedly took off after her, but she agilely wove through the market stalls and lost them in the crowd. Now, she could rest in the dense, cool, forest for the last hours of daylight and enjoy her treasures. However, her security would be short-lived; by darkness she would have to find a safe place to sleep. This was her third day of freedom.

As a slave, she had received adequate food on the olive oil plantation east of Antioch where she had lived. But she had constantly dreamed of a run for freedom. Three days ago, she had not really planned escape, but her owner had been distracted, and the opportunity to slip away presented itself. She last saw him leaning unsteadily on a stool while drinking with a business partner. She had feigned interest in some produce. He was unconcerned when she wandered farther away. She took one more glance back and then quickly ducked behind a building. Her owner must not have missed her for some time. In a maze of narrow corridors, she heard no

Rhoda, the Servant Girl Who Persisted

commotion behind her as she quietly picked up her steps. She did not attract any attention. The getaway turned out to be the easy part.

Once on the run, a host of unforeseen dangers would be a part of her daily life. If she were captured, anyone could return her to her owner . . . if they could find out his identity. She would never tell. She would die first. Her owner was not suffering a big loss, because he had never paid anything for her, so he probably would not try very hard to find her. Twelve years ago, although she was not sure how old she was, another slave had been tasked with carrying out orders to leave a baby on a rocky cliff. If a baby was less than perfect, inconvenient, or born female, the baby's father or master would determine if this offspring was worth keeping. Unwanted infants were left on a lonely ledge to die of hunger, cold, or be eaten by wild animals. However, if the gods looked on an abandoned baby with favor, the crying, starving infant may be rescued. Some plantation owners would send a trusted slave to look for abandoned babies, even baby girls. If the baby had a lusty cry and was found, a master might raise the child to do agricultural labor. In many cases, death may have been the better alternative. The girl had been such a foundling. She knew only one more piece of information about herself. She had been born on the Greek island of Rhodes.

Now, once again in her life, her survival was dependent on the gods.

She had heard about Daphne's Grove. This was a place, it was said, where the authorities could not easily capture escaped slaves. It was a forested safe place, or sanctuary, along the river: a magical hideaway with springs and waterfalls. But she had to get there first. Luckily, it wasn't too far from where she had slipped away from her master.

She caught her breath the first time she entered into the shade of Daphne's Grove. Above the treetops, a huge statue of Apollo loomed overhead. The statue was surrounded by many people, each with a desperate wish. They were chanting, praying, and making offerings. The gods do not hear humans unless they received an offering. She had nothing, or at least she was not going to offer what little she had and so she had not expected anything from Apollo. Worshippers often left food offerings, which, if she was clever, she could snatch. She hoped Apollo did not mind, but the gods had abandoned her since the day she was rescued as an infant. She doubted that her little indiscretion would change her fate.

According to the ancient stories she had heard, Apollo had seduced Daphne in this very grove. However, Daphne did not wish his attention and fled his advances. The pursuit came to a cruel end for Apollo. In this grove, the Mother Earth turned Daphne into a laurel tree. Apollo took leaves from the laurel tree and made a wreath for his head as consolation for his lost love.

The now-escaped slave girl loved the Greek stories of ancient gods, even though the gods did not return her devotion. To be in the location of such an important event would normally be thrilling, but she did not have the luxury to dwell on it. On the first day of freedom, she fell asleep in the dappled shade of a laurel by a waterfall, and so lost track of time. Shadows were long when she woke, and she knew her rest was over. At night, the activities in the temple of Apollo became unsavory, and the danger to a girl would be great. Going outside the sacred grove was the only alternative.

On that first night of freedom, she climbed a tree for a sleeping place. Because she had spent most of her life picking olives, sleeping in a tree was a natural solution to her. The rats would not climb up into a tree and, in addition, most people kept their eyes to the ground as they went about their affairs. The neighborhood around the Daphne Grove was forested with big trees. The nights remained warm, and she could sleep fitfully in the fork of the branches. It was a good solution; it had worked well for the first two nights because few people thought to look up. When nightfall approached, she slipped away from Daphne's Grove and retook her safe sleeping place in the branches of the big trees.

The third morning, she awoke suddenly from her semi-dozing state. The tree was violently shaking. She tumbled from the limbs and caught herself hanging by her arms from the lowest branch. She was eye level with a large man. Someone had finally cast his eyes heavenward!

"Is this the little fruit thief?"

Her heart crushed. She was doomed. She tried to force her grip on the branch to relax. She hoped to drop to the ground and make a desperate run for it, but her fingers were locked. Then the man grasped her by the waist and gently set her on her feet. She could only stand and stare.

"So now, what should I do with you, so conveniently plucked from a tree?"

"Oh," she stammered. "Forgive me, I didn't mean to be in your tree." She sunk to the ground at his feet and started to sob.

"Well, to think this could be my tree. Come now child, get up, and stop blubbering."

Rhoda, the Servant Girl Who Persisted

She got to her feet, and he wiped her tears with the sleeves of his garment, sort of like she always imagined a father would do, and smoothed down her ragged clothes. Was this Apollo answering her prayers?

"Now child, tell me what on earth you were doing in that tree?" He took her hand and started walking her down the street. Strangely, she did not feel like pulling out of his grasp.

"Well, I needed a place to sleep . . . and there were some olives to eat . . . and I couldn't stay in the Daphne's Grove . . . and I escaped from my owner. . ." Oh, no. That is not what she should have said. Now she was in even bigger trouble. This man would try to return her for a reward.

"What was that last thing you said?"

"Oh, nothing, I should have got down from the tree sooner to get back to my home." The lies were piling up.

"You don't look to me like you have a home. Now tell me, is someone looking for you. Do your parents know where you are?" The man turned toward her and looked her straight in the face. Somehow she trusted him. Anyway, now she had no choice.

"I am an escaped slave; I just want to be free. If my owner finds me, I will be dead. Please sir, help me hide; and do you have any food?" She immediately regretted the last statement. She had bigger problems, at that moment, than finding food.

"Now calm down. I'll fix you up so you won't be recognized, and we will get to the meeting place of the Jesus followers. Pretend you are my daughter and don't cry."

"A daughter? I can be your daughter, not a slave?" He smiled at her, and she saw something for the first time ever in her life: eyes that beamed affection toward her.

"We have rescued a few lost sheep like you, just come along. Now tell me about yourself, what is your name?"

She stammered out her very short story.

"Rhoda it will be. Rhoda is your name because you were born on Rhodes; besides, it means 'rose' and you are pretty as a rose—or at least you will be when cleaned up."

"Pretty as a rose," this is getting better and better, she thought. Now she felt like Daphne must have felt when Apollo pursued her.

"Are you Apollo?" Rhoda asked him.

The man let out a hearty laugh. This was the first time she had heard such genuine laughter. The fear that froze her heart was melting rapidly.

They walked together through many back alleys to a section of Antioch that she did not know. The houses were grander than that of her former owner. Could she dare hope to become a slave in this household? They entered a courtyard where they interrupted a group of people who were breaking bread and passing a cup around at a table.

"Barnabas, you really were determined to seek out some of the Jewish leaders today who live near Daphne's Grove," one of them said to the man.

"So, what did you find at Daphne's Grove?" asked another with too much curiosity.

"I found a lovely young lady who is convinced that I am Apollo," Barnabas said. He was still amused at the thought. "She is steeped in the Greek stories, so we have some teaching to do, but the saving Spirit has already started to work."

At first Rhoda did not understand this new community and how they welcomed her. They called each other brothers and sisters, and treated her like a daughter. She trusted them immediately because they talked to her and didn't just order her to work. She had only known of masters and slaves before; she never knew that people could act any other way. They were different and she wanted to know more about them.

"Why do you call yourselves Christians? What kind of new thinking is this?" The questions poured out of her. "I have never heard of Christians; who is Christ? You do not seem to be interested in Apollo and Daphne very much."

These people patiently tried to calm some of her fears.

"Yes, this is all very confusing. I wonder how long can I stay here?" she asked herself.

Rhoda soon found herself smothered with food, a bath, clean clothes, and a safe place to sleep. Her questions were answered with deeds and not words. She began to understand how Christians were different. They worshiped a man called Jesus who had been crucified by the Romans only about ten years earlier in Jerusalem. But Jesus was not only a man, but the living God, unlike the Greek gods who were only stones. Jesus rose from the dead three days after being crucified and now lived in heaven, but also was alive in the people who believed in him. Barnabas, who had witnessed those events, had come to Antioch to preach about Jesus to the Jews. Others listened as well, including Greeks, like herself. Some were even former slaves. Was she still a slave? That she did not know. She did not want to ask. She also did not want to escape.

Rhoda, the Servant Girl Who Persisted

During the next days of her new freedom she began to feel whole. This new freedom was far beyond just being free of the hardships she had known before. A great burden was being lifted from her shoulders, her hands, and her heart.

A NEW LIFE

It was the day of her baptism. Several weeks had passed since she ran for freedom. She told her new friends and Barnabas that she wanted to be a Christ-follower and become a part of this group called Christians. They brought her to a small chapel in a cave carved into the mountainside. Her new white robe was beautiful. Not long ago she would have thought that she looked just like Daphne, but Greek gods were in her past. Those gods were stone silent and did not care for her. Jesus was different. He cared about her even though she did not bring him anything but her love. Her new Christian friends showed her what Jesus was like by their care. She did not bring them anything either, but they gave her everything they had and accepted her totally.

"I baptize you, Rhoda, in the name of the Father, Son, and Holy Spirit," Barnabas said. These were the words Christians used in baptisms. "There is neither Jew nor Greek, slave nor free, male nor female, for you are all one in Christ Jesus."

The cold spring water caused her to shiver. The baptism was quite a graphic way to demonstrate that her old life had been washed away. Through baptism she had experienced a new birth. She shuddered at the thought of her first birth, but now, for the first time, she was free of her past. She did not quite understand how she fit in this new family; they assured her she was no longer a slave. The new Christians, who mostly came from Jewish traditions, worshiped the Christian God who was not made of stone. This God was invisible, yet felt. Together, they were leaving behind old customs and starting new ones. They tried new foods. During her old life, she sometimes worked in the kitchen between harvest seasons. She prepared meals she had learned there, dishes her new brothers and sisters had never tasted. But they eagerly tried what she made. She was just settling in to all this newness when yet another change loomed on the horizon.

One day Barnabas mentioned to her, "I'm going back to Jerusalem; I need to do some explaining to James, the brother of Jesus, and the apostles at the Temple. Would you like to see Jerusalem?"

"I cannot imagine such a place," Rhoda stammered. "The language is Aramaic and the food is all Jewish?"

"Actually, you will find many customs familiar to a Greek person, but it certainly is the home of the Jews and the place where Jesus lived. You would live with my aunt, Mary Mark, who has a large household and could use a servant. No, not a slave, a servant, and when you are older, you will be a free woman."

"Father Barnabas," as Rhoda called him, "All this change is making me dizzy, but I would love to find my real home and I think it will be in Jerusalem."

The city of Jerusalem lay golden in the sunset on the final day of their travel from Antioch; Rhoda indeed had left an old world for a new.

"That must be the Temple of the Jews. It is different than the temples of the Greeks, because there are no images of gods," she exclaimed to Barnabas. "No wonder the Jews love it so. Will we visit it soon?"

"Yes, it is beautiful, but it is not really ours anymore," Barnabas explained ominously. "I have important news to deliver there, and as a Greek convert to Christianity you are part of it, Rhoda." At that time, she did not understand the remark. "Herod Agrippa runs everything now. He says he is a Jew, but he just pleases the Romans. He does not understand the Christians and has killed some of our leaders. While I was gone, James, one of the original twelve apostles of Jesus, was beheaded." That news sent a certain chill over her initial enthusiasm. They quickly arrived at the grand house of Mary Mark.

"So glad to see you, my nephew," Mary exclaimed, and then she turned to the Greek servant girl. "Rhoda, welcome, you are pretty as a rose," she hugged her warmly. His aunt was just like Barnabas, but why did her new name "Rhoda" catch so much attention? She quickly made herself at home.

"Rhoda, fetch more olive oil from the cellar, we have unexpected visitors." She heard such orders all day but she liked her new place.

"Rhoda, be sure to taste it before you pour it on the greens, sometimes it spoils," the older servant recommended. That was an order Rhoda obeyed gladly. The olive oil was different in Jerusalem from that in Antioch and needed a hint of tarragon for sweetening.

"We never add citrus to the marinade, Rhoda," they cautioned her. Instead of becoming defensive of her practices in the kitchen, she remembered the words Barnabas had spoken at her baptism, "In Christ there is no Jew or Greek."

The servants talked among themselves in the kitchen, and occasionally their differences would come out. Everyone had to learn new ways.

"What are we supposed to do about separating dairy products from the meat?" one servant asked. "I remember when the dietary laws were very strictly followed. How can we just give up the old traditions so fast?" another servant wondered.

"Should Jews and Gentiles even be eating together? And I will never eat such unclean food as pork," declared an older servant who was having a very hard time adjusting.

"Hey, I'm here," Rhoda burst out without thinking. "I'm Greek; I'm a Gentile and a believer in Jesus. If I had a small bit of pork in a thin milk broth when I was a slave, it was a feast."

"You are right, Rhoda Pretty as a Rose, you are certainly one of us, even with your different ways. It is just a matter of getting to know a person," another servant girl added. "Pretty as a Rose" became her last name, since she did not have any other.

Bold Girls Speak

A KNOCK AT THE DOOR

One day, big strong Barnabas, whose hearty laugh would ring through the house, rushed back to Mary's house in tears. "Herod Agrippa has chained Peter in prison! He may be executed as James the apostle was." Rhoda felt dread well up inside her; Peter was a regular visitor in Mary Mark's house. She listened eagerly to all of his stories. Mary Mark's son, John Mark, wrote down everything he knew about the life of Jesus on pages of papyrus.

Mary gave Rhoda a new assignment. "You keep the gate locked and only allow people you know to come in. We are all in danger." For the first time Rhoda wished she had stayed in Antioch. Those first days with the Christians were such a sweet memory, but they had fairly warned her of the dangers of following Jesus. She did not expect it to be so dangerous so fast. Now her assignment was to keep the door shut and carefully question everyone who knocked.

Mary's house was a favorite gathering place for the Christians. Rhoda knew the usual friends who entered as they covered their tear-streaked faces. "Dear God in heaven, please deliver our brother Peter from prison." She heard these words repeatedly for several nights as the Christians gathered at Mary's house.

"Dear Lord, I am only a girl, a servant, and of all people a Greek, but I know you hear me pray. Bring Peter back to us," she prayed.

Darkness fell and a cold wind blew. She may have been dozing; she thought it was just the wind. Suddenly she heard a faint but very insistent knock at the door. Her heart raced as she reached for the latch. After all, who could be there? Friend or foe? Rhoda opened it a crack and looked out.

"I am Peter, let me in!" The dark figure standing in the moonlight urgently whispered. She recognized his voice; her heart stopped. She was so astounded she quickly shut the door again.

"Peter is at the door!" she gasped. She raced from the courtyard and burst into the house. The gathered people raised their heads from prayer and opened their dazed eyes. "It is Peter, he just knocked at the door," she exclaimed.

"You are a crazy girl." They laughed at her, and it was not a funny laugh. It was a laugh of ridicule. "This is a very cruel joke," they added.

"You don't believe me. He is there; I saw him. I heard him."

"You are seeing his angel." His angel? What did they mean by that? Was she not responsible enough to know the difference between a real person and a ghost?

"Well, let him in and bring him here, if he is really there." The group seemed willing to indulge her in her fantasy. She would be horribly humiliated if they proved her wrong.

She went back through the courtyard, hardly trusting her senses. What if her imagination was being overactive? Would Peter still be there? Now the knocking was more insistent.

"Do I have to break the door down? Finally, let me in, my girl." Peter wedged through the door as soon as she cracked it, and he fell on the floor in a heap. The rest of the group quickly gathered around when they heard the commotion. They grasped him with tears of joy and helped him to his feet. They handed him a hot cup of broth to drink.

"My beloved ones, I have a miraculous story to tell," Peter started his story. "I am free! Many guards were watching me to be sure I could not escape, and then an angel suddenly lit up the gloomy dungeon and said, 'Get up and get dressed quickly!' It was a miracle. The chains fell from my hands and feet! I walked right through a gate and out of the prison to freedom. An angel led me safely through the streets of Jerusalem. And then the angel disappeared abruptly into nowhere."

"Why do angels keep coming up?" She wondered if she had an angel for a friend.

Peter's story of escape to freedom held the assembled Christians spellbound until late into the night. They had to let Peter go again before the light of day. He was insistent that he had to get out of the city to a place unknown to the authorities because he was in danger. Even Mary's household was in danger because Roman soldiers would come looking for him. After many "Godspeeds" and prayers, Rhoda reluctantly opened the gate for him. Now he was her friend, too.

WHEN FRIENDS ARE CRUEL

Rhoda started to make her long-overdue climb to the sleeping loft for the servants. This life with the Christians would never be boring.

"Rhoda, I have a favor to ask you," Mary's voice called after her. "Someone needs to go to James the Elder's house to tell him that Peter is safe. I want him to know the whole story. Will you come with me?" Rhoda's heart leaped with the rare opportunity to talk to her mistress Mary Mark. "Get yourself a warm wrap; the sun will be rising."

"We were pretty hard on you last night, weren't we?" Mary's kind voice asked after they had walked a ways.

"Yes, all of you should have believed me when I announced that Peter was there," Rhoda stammered and then immediately swallowed her words. Why did she always blurt out exactly what first came to her mind without thinking?

"I mean, I really should have let Peter into the courtyard right away instead of slamming the door in his face and making him stand outside in the street," Rhoda said, quickly regained her composure. "After all, imagine, he was just rescued from prison by angels. What an absolute miracle, and then to think, he could have been caught again by Herod's guards right outside your gate." Rhoda shuddered to think how horrible that would have been, and totally her fault!

"We were all worried and praying so hard," Mary reassured her. "We should have shown stronger faith that our prayers would be answered, and we shouldn't have called you 'crazy' when you told us Peter was standing at the door."

"Well, now I am just beginning to think about it, with all the excitement and everything, it hadn't occurred to me that it was unfair," Rhoda replied. Actually, it had bothered Rhoda quite a bit. Considering the miraculous events, she really did not think her hurt feelings mattered that much. But then a tumble of thoughts vexed her, and words came pouring out. "I like my adopted name quite a lot, 'Rhoda,' it has a nice sound; it still shows my identity as a Greek, which I don't have to give up as a Christian. Yes, no one should call me 'crazy girl'; I have a real name. So why were they so quick to call me 'crazy'? I have lived as lowly as a slave, but never as low as the beggars who are called 'crazy.'"

"It is hard for some people to accept those who are from a lower class, or female, or another nationality, as equal in ability. I promise it will not happen again," Mary said, taking her hand.

Rhoda, the Servant Girl Who Persisted

This apology from Mary lifted a weight off Rhoda's shoulders; words failed her just this one time. They admired the sunrise as they made their way to the house of James. Rhoda was amazed at the opportunity to meet him.

"Tell me about James, the half brother of Jesus," Rhoda asked, for she never lacked for questions.

"He is the leader of the Christians in Jerusalem, and you can ask him a few questions about Jesus. But I also am interested that he meets you, our Rhoda, a Greek rose, formerly a slave from Antioch."

"Can I tell him Peter's story of gaining freedom from the chains of the prison?" Rhoda wondered aloud. "Remember how he told us that he would be tried for execution in the morning? Then in one blinding flash he is freed by an angel. The very next minute he meets a servant girl who won't let him in the house!" She could laugh about it now.

POINTS TO PONDER ABOUT RHODA

The times were very hard for the early Christians in Jerusalem after Jesus' resurrection and ascension into heaven. They were horribly persecuted under the reign of evil Roman kings. Many died as martyrs. Others, like Peter, were arrested and imprisoned. Meanwhile the Christian community, as it has done throughout the centuries since, gathered in the home of a believer to pray together on behalf of their loved ones in trouble.

On this occasion, prayers were answered for Peter. He thought he was in a dream as the angel guided him out of the prison and into the city streets of Jerusalem. Then as fast as the angel appeared, he disappeared, leaving Peter very astounded at his sudden freedom. He went to the house where he had been many times before, the meeting place of his fellow Christ-believers who had gathered to pray for him. This house had been a sanctuary for many over the years, and he knew this would be a safe place he could reach quickly.

Here is where he met our *Bold Girl*, Rhoda. How did she become a servant in this household? Who was she and where was she from? The story about her being born in Rhodes is imaginary, but possible. Slaves were often given pet names that reflected something about them.

The Scripture passage gives us little information concerning her age. But it is apparent that she was not old enough so that the others in the household took her very seriously. It is also obvious that she had already overcome difficult times in order to learn the persistence that she needed that night when no one would believe her. Maybe her behavior in her excitement reminds you of yourself, or of your friends. Have you ever felt that people would not listen to you just because you happen to be young or different in other ways?

Imagine Peter's feelings! He had just experienced an incredible rescue from prison, which could not possibly have really sunk in yet, and now he is at the door of a familiar house, desperate to catch his breath and collapse in safety. The door is tentatively opened a crack. He hears a gasp, and then the door is slammed in his face by a young servant girl! Angels one minute—servant girls the next! Servant girls had figured uncomfortably in Peter's life before. Remember that night of Jesus' trial before he was crucified? Another *Bold Girls* story included Peter's encounter with the servant girls in the courtyard of Caiaphas. Now, Peter is in despair, ecstasy the next, and now back in despair—all within a few minutes. Do your feelings change that fast sometimes?

Do you recognize yourself in Rhoda's behavior? How often do you react before thinking? Rhoda's excitement got the best of her, too, when she heard Peter's voice but did not let him in the house. Peter surely forgave her lack of hospitality that night as soon as he was safe inside.

Peter, of course, is the name we usually remember in this story. A few words are sometimes said about the hospitable woman, Mary Mark, who led a house church that was a haven for the early Christians. But rarely is much thought given to Rhoda, the servant girl. For some reason Rhoda's name is especially remembered in this momentous event that has been recorded in the book of Acts. We should take note of any lessons she teaches us.

Rhoda is a glimpse into a real human character that survived and thrived in the circumstances in which she was placed. How we would love to know more about her. It is a lot of fun to imagine the things she experienced. This *Bold Girls* story contains greatly contrasting events: a determined pagan girl who flees to freedom, a loving embrace of a Christian community, a journey to a strange land, a miraculous escape from prison with the help of an angel, and finally an illustration of human frailty in the person of Rhoda, a servant girl. We cannot help but love Rhoda!

The character of Mary Mark is taken directly from the Bible passage in Acts 12:12. Her son, John Mark, is known as the writer of the Gospel of Mark, which was written perhaps a decade later. In this *Bold Girls* story, he

Rhoda, the Servant Girl Who Persisted

is already taking notes and gathering his information for his Gospel. The note-taking part of the story is fictional, but it is easy to imagine that he has started to write down information so he will not forget the important events. Barnabas does not actually appear in Acts 12, but he is known from other biblical passages—Acts 4:36; 9:27; 13:1–3; and Acts 11:24—where he is called a "good man, full of the Holy Spirit and faith." In Colossians 4:10 he is introduced as the cousin of Mark, so that would make Mark's mother the aunt of Barnabas. He was also known to be the preaching partner of Paul.

The city of Antioch has no connection with the story of Rhoda from Acts 12, but this city is mentioned in Acts 11 and 13. It was an important city in the activities of the early Christ followers. It was in Antioch that they were first called "Christians," and a cave can still be visited that was the location of Christian worship since very early times. Barnabas had a close connection with Antioch, where he and Paul started out on their missionary journeys.

Many cultural and historical details have been added to this *Bold Girls* story. These details are not included in the passage from Acts 12. However, a study of the events and problems that the early Christians faced will help you in understanding many passages of the New Testament. Indeed, some of the challenges of those early days of Christianity are illustrated in this *Bold Girls* story.

A big issue at this time was how the first Christians, who were from Jewish backgrounds, would get along with non-Jewish people who had converted to Christianity. Jesus and his disciples were all Jews, but many memorable stories in the Old Testament and in the New Testament are about how people who were not Jewish but loved the Jewish God. Many New Testament stories also describe people hearing about Jesus and believing in him. Jesus had a special interest in reaching people who were outside the Jewish faith. Examples include the Roman centurion (Matt 8:5–13), the Canaanite woman (Matt 15:21–28), the Samaritan woman of John 4, and many more.

The Jews, whose stories are known from the Old Testament, had a long history of staying to themselves. They lived separated from other people that they called "Gentiles," and had many customs that made them very obviously different. They did not eat with non-Jews, would not go into their houses, and considered everyone who was not Jewish "unclean." When Jews started having contact with non-Jews, conflict occurred with the Jewish leadership as they tried to figure out how to worship together, how to follow Jesus as a community of believers, and even how to eat together. When non-Jews started believing in Jesus, those who were ethnically Jewish had a hard time accepting these converts to Christianity. Jesus taught that all people who believed in him were to be accepted as equals, as stated in the baptism quote, which was later recorded by Paul in Galatians 3:28. Later, the many letters of Paul are heavily concerned with how the old Jewish laws were no longer important and how new customs should take their place. In this *Bold Girls* story, we see how Rhoda came to be baptized. This was a new practice at the time, and it replaced the Jewish custom of circumcision.

The story of Rhoda illustrates how the ethnic Jews had to get used to eating with non-Jews. Together, they learned that all foods were good to eat. An important turning point in dietary matters was Peter's vision in Acts 10; but even earlier Jesus said that his followers could eat anything (Matt 15:10). Jesus also ate with non-Jews, which made the Jewish authorities angry.

From Acts 12, there is no way of knowing if Rhoda really was a Greek girl, but considering her name, it is a possibility. The rubbing points between the Jewish servants and a Greek newcomer is a small example of the kind of conflict that took place when these two groups of people, Jews and Gentiles, came together. It was usually much more intense, as we know from Paul's letters.

Several other items from this *Bold Girls* story are worth noting and help to understand the world of the Bible. The Greco-Roman empire, in which Jesus lived, practiced many different religions. Most people at that time would have known and worshipped the Greek gods, who they believed completely controlled their lives. These gods had to be worshipped in their temples in particular ways so they would be kept happy and bless the people. Some of the so-called worship was very wicked.

Today, what we know as stories from Greek mythology are exciting to read for fun, such as Homer's Odyssey and the stories of the Greek gods. Ruins of the temples to Greek gods can still be seen today throughout the Mediterranean countries. It is true that outside of Antioch there was a forested area with waterfalls that surrounded a temple to Apollo. Escaped slaves really could find refuge in the grove known as Daphne's Grove. It is also tragically true that unwanted babies would be left to die in a lonely place. Fathers really did have the authority to decide to get rid of their own offspring. The early Christians rescued these helpless babies and raised

Rhoda, the Servant Girl Who Persisted

them as their own. The times in which the Bible stories took place are very much different from the twenty-first century. It is important to try to understand these differences in order to interpret the Bible accurately.

QUESTIONS FOR DISCUSSION

1. Have your friends ever laughed at you? Jesus may have experienced a similar feeling when he was betrayed and deserted by his disciples in the Garden of Gethsemane at the hour of his greatest need, right before he was crucified. Sometimes we can learn about Jesus through our own feelings. Jesus was human as well as God in his time on earth. He felt the same emotions that we do!

2. Think about the meaning of sanctuary. You may refer to a room of your church as a sanctuary. A church should be a sanctuary or a sort of safe place from the dangers and worries of the world. In the imaginary story of Rhoda, she found a sanctuary in a place of pagan worship, but it wasn't a true sanctuary because she was not safe to stay there at night. Christians find sanctuary with Jesus where they are free from fear.

3. At the time that this *Bold Girls* story takes place, the message of Jesus was spreading from people who were originally Jewish to the Gentiles, who were outsiders. Did this merging of cultures happen without controversy and conflict? What often happens when people who are different are brought into a group of close friends?

4. Rhoda did her job in the best way she knew, even though she was the lowest ranked person in the household. How do you use your talents in your church at the age you are now?

RELATED CULTURAL AND HISTORICAL QUESTIONS TO EXPLORE

1. Try to place the events of this *Bold Girls* story into a timeline. This story took place at about ad 44. Jesus was crucified in about ad 33. What has been happening in these years, both in the Roman world and in the history of the church?

2. James, one of the original disciples of Christ, was martyred at this time. How did the other apostles die? Many women and men, boys and girls died cruelly because of their faith. Do you know any of their names and stories?

3. What other encounters does Peter have with servant girls? (Remember, servant girls were present on the night of Peter's denial and at the raising of Jarius's daughter.) We know that Peter had a mother-in-law, so he was married. Could he have had a daughter of his own? The *Bold Girls* story, "The Girl Whose Hand Jesus Touched," includes a fictional character who is the daughter of Peter. A legend exists that Peter had a daughter named Petronella who was a first-century martyr in Rome.

4. What are your dreams for work in the church and your occupation as you get older? What are the jobs girls and boys can do to help in the work of spreading the gospel? Are boys and girls encouraged to develop different gifts in your church? Do boys and girls receive different spiritual gifts?

5. Does God give gifts to people determined by their color of skin, nationality, or gender?

SUGGESTED TOPICS OF DISCUSSION FOR TEACHERS AND PARENTS OF OLDER STUDENTS

1. According to the fictional parts of this *Bold Girls* story, Rhoda was a "rescued" baby. What happens to children who are unwanted in the ancient world? In the modern world? How were abortion and infanticide practiced then and now? How were Christians different in ancient times and now? How are Christians different from the prevailing culture in ancient times and now?

2. Why were girls less desirable than boys in the first century? Does discrimination against girls still occur today?

3. What were the names of the Greek and Roman gods? Look up their stories and mythologies.

4. What were the pagan worship practices of the Greeks and Romans? Depending on the maturity of the class, details of pagan worship such as child sacrifice and temple prostitution could be discussed. Emperor

Rhoda, the Servant Girl Who Persisted

worship was also required in the Roman Empire. How did the early Christians fare in the Roman Empire?

5. Research slavery in the Roman Empire and where slavery still exists today.

6. A common belief at the time this *Bold Girls* story takes place was that every believer was given a special guardian angel that looked like the person they were protecting. Apparently, the people at Mary's house that night believed Rhoda was seeing Peter's guardian angel. What do you think about having a guardian angel?

The Girl Who Found Her Own Voice

ACTS 16:16–40

A NIGHT OF TELLING FORTUNES

A LEATHER FLAP BLOCKED the gusty wind from blowing into her cave, located on the outskirts of Philippi. Inside, smoky oil lamps gently swung from the soot-covered ceiling and illuminated a young fortune-teller who was hunched over a table. The silky, long, white sleeves of her robe fell back to reveal gold bangle bracelets on her wrists and glittering rings. She stared at a precious crystal flask containing water, oil, and other secret ingredients that she set into a swirling motion by the flick of her wrist. In the middle of her forehead, a jeweled amulet sparkled as she intently contemplated the smoky mixture. Her pursed lips made a slight hissing sound when a vision became clear; she was seeing into someone's future. An impatient shuffling of footsteps outside the cave interrupted her concentration. She stole a glance at the leather flap.;

Mercy, more patrons are standing in line. How many more hours of fortune-telling await me before I can leave this cave? My face feels plastered into an empty fake smile. How much longer can I endure this endless charade, which continues until late every night!

She longed to roll her shoulders and massage her neck a moment. The anxious man facing her strained to read her eyes and catch the slightest hint of what she might be glimpsing. He was weary from a day of traveling by foot from the seaport. In his desperation, he gladly paid a month's wages to the man at the cave entrance to get relief from the torment of not knowing his son's fate as a soldier in the latest battle. Little was he aware that the

The Girl Who Found Her Own Voice

young fortune-teller at that moment was not intently penetrating the deepest secrets of magical realms to determine if his only son still lived.

"Step right up! For a small fee, learn your fortune from the amazing young priestess, recently initiated in Delphi, instructed in the secret ways of the oracle. Why wait to find out if your olive oil shipment is safe, if your woman is faithful, or if that scoundrel of a brother-in-law stole your goat?" A man with a snake coiled around one arm hollered to a small crowd of desperate souls who had gathered around, long after the marketplace was empty. "You have the look of a man with a burden that needs to be lifted. Bring your worries here! Don't plan your next business venture until you've heard the whole truth of what your future holds!" He took little rolls of papyrus or lead from the customers, each with the person's deepest wishes and fears inscribed upon it. He also took their money.

These words rang in the ears of the fortune-teller's hapless customer as he held his breath to hear every word she would mutter. Some vague shapes began to form in the oil and water mixture as the two elements separated to form wispy streams.

"Is she seeing the face of my son? Is he living or dead? Where is he? Is he calling for help?" The man's pulse raced.

Oh yes, back to the business at hand. She jerked her thoughts back to the present and the nagging line outside. She narrowed her eyes and concentrated on the furrowed brow of the tall, thin man seated in front of her. The crinkles around his eyes appeared to be formed by a life of real concerns for those he loved. Hmmm . . . visions were coming into focus.

So much misery in this world! I really wish I could erase some of the dread from his face. Stop! Dismiss those thoughts. I learned long time ago to maintain an emotional distance from my costumers. Okay, I am going to tell him something encouraging. What kind of story can I tell him that will lighten his load, if only temporarily? How will he ever know the truth? I tell the patrons what they want to hear, unless I do not like them. On a whim, I may decide to endorse their worst fears. If I must endure a curse, this is the one redeeming factor. I am powerful! I can bring tears of joy or howls of desperation just by muttering a few words.

"Oh, I see something," she said with phony drama. "It is becoming clear to me, Spirit of Python, speak your mysteries, quickly now, clearer! Oh, this is it! Yes, sir, I see a young man, with a scar on his face. He is tall and thin . . . is your son tall and thin? Oh yes, that is him. He lives . . ."

She did not remember what more she said to the man. He left rejoicing and exclaiming her praises to those still waiting in line. Throughout the evening, she repeated the same act. She sighed wearily between customers. Countless variations of the same story kept the hours interesting for her amusement. Over the years, she had developed an astonishing imagination, but she was also a keen observer of human nature. She could tell volumes about people by watching their gestures, hands, and the movements of their eyes. It was like looking into their minds.

Yes, I am remarkably intuitive about people, she reassured herself. *I have had this uncanny ability for as long as I can remember. I felt this difference even at a very young age . . . did I learn it, or is there something more?* That brief thought sent a shiver down her spine, which she promptly dismissed.

A black marble obelisk stood at her left side, the so-called "navel of the world." Of course, this was not the real one. That was in Delphi, but the patrons did not care about such details. She sat on a tripod, a three-legged stool, so she was considerably more elevated than those seeking her counsel. Her cave was an imitation of the cave of the oracle in Delphi. Piles of musty scrolls lay in a corner; her pet owl dozed to her right on a perch. Outside were crates of squawking, small fowl. If a patron could afford it, a bird could be purchased; she would ring its neck and slit open the breast. Then she would examine its organs and study patterns in the intestines to divine the future. It was distasteful work. Thankfully, not too many customers were willing to pay for the privilege, but her pet owl was glad for the leftovers.

"So, my pretty young lady," a sailor before her leered suggestively. "Are we going to find out how rich I will be when my smuggled goods are sold? You better be worth every cent."

Smugly, she opened a pouch hanging from her belt. She removed two stones with spots engraved on each of the six sides and skillfully threw them with a flick of her wrist. They rolled to a rest on the table before her. Little did he know that she had already determined his future. In a few minutes, he cowered out of the cavern, dragging his feet as though he had a heavy burden on his shoulders.

The Girl Who Found Her Own Voice

WHO KNOWS WHO I AM?

The heavenly constellations had moved across the sky by the time she crawled under the blankets they gave her for a bed in the back room of a rented house. She was a slave; they owned her. She held in her memory the number of times she had been bought and sold, but she did not know her age. Her value was the money she brought into the jar of the couple who owned her; from the patrons who sought her fortune-telling ability. Money did not have any meaning for her, but she understood its value—most of her customers wanted more of it. She was more interested in what her own future held for her. While she predicted fortunes for paying strangers, she silently searched for answers about her own. Her knowledge of astrology was useless in her own case, especially since she did not know her own birth date.

Did the mysterious woman who gave birth to her still remember a baby daughter on her birthday? How desperate was her father who earned a sudden windfall when he sold his child? She knew full well why they gave her up. When her condition became apparent, there was only one possible solution for her parents, and that was to sell their child to the highest bidder.

Most mornings she thankfully slept late. She enjoyed a few hours wandering throughout the forum to observe the people. No one suspected her other identity; she just looked like a usual slave girl. Each evening, as the moon rose, she transformed herself into a different person when she dressed in her work robe of fine white linen. A clove of garlic hung in a bag between her breasts. She slipped a big stone, the "evil eye," on her ring finger. Impatient patrons had already formed lines when she entered the cave at sunset. Nightly, the charade began all over again.

This life was tolerable, and actually had some advantages. However, deep inside, something else possessed her. She lived every day in terror of one unpredictable torment that would interrupt this routine. The memory alone caused sweat to bead up on her forehead.

Someday it will kill me. This was her most horrible fear. Without warning, although a nearby dog may bark at her furiously, the old demon, the Python of Apollo, would grip her in a spasm until she fell helpless to the ground. Screaming unintelligible sounds until she was hoarse and exhausted, she flailed away at anything that came near her. Crowds of people stared at her agony and beckoned others to come and gawk. Her owners would grin with greediness when they saw the Spirit of Python begin to work its spell.

"Hear the latest prophesy coming directly from the underworld, from the giant serpent killed by Apollo at Delphi," shouted her owners into the crowds. The spectacle was accompanied by the clatter of more coins falling into the jar as her owners spun fantastic lies about what they determined the spirit was saying through her. She regained consciousness hours later, rolled up in a fetal position, filthy with the dust from the market square. Her hands and feet would be bound up so she could not injure herself.

"Like they really care about me," she spoke out with scorn. Often they would stick a rag in her mouth until she almost choked. After all, if she bit off her tongue, what use would she be to them? When her body finally relaxed, her mind would be in a trance for hours, or more recently, even days. Then, her owners would announce that her fortune-telling ability had returned with enhanced clarity.

STRANGE VISITORS IN PHILIPPI

One day, among the many people crowding the marketplace of Philippi, two unusual travelers attracted her attention. One was a short man and the other man was taller; they reminded her of Zeus and Apollo. She overheard gossip concerning the travelers. They were Jews from Judea, and they were attracting attention with a new message about Jesus who had been crucified in Jerusalem about twenty years earlier. People with this background had not yet visited her cave. She first followed the visitors out of curiosity, but soon felt compelled to hear their whole message. They talked of a "one true God" and the "way of salvation." Could they have knowledge of a truth unlike the phony truths she spun for money?

The Girl Who Found Her Own Voice

That night she mouthed the usual fantasies for her patrons. But a dissonance was creeping into her mind, even while her hands habitually repeated the rituals. To whom could she pray?

Later that night, she wandered through the forum of Philippi back to a fine house that her owners could afford because of her earnings. Every nook and cranny of the shops in the forum were packed with stone images of gods. A religion or cult existed for every need to suit every person. Some people even thought she was a goddess! She knew she did not have any power to change events; were these many other gods equally as powerless as she was? On her nighttime walk back to her bed, she again searched the stars for answers. But now she had new pieces to the puzzle. These men called themselves servants of the one true God and servants of Jesus, his son. They said that they knew the way to salvation. What did this mean? She was compelled to know more.

She awoke as usual late the next morning. She searched the marketplace for the mysterious strangers called Jews who preached this new message. A crowd had gathered around them near a stall where vivid purple fabrics were flapping in the wind. The young fortune-teller edged forward to hear the shorter man speak. "Do everything so that you may become children of God in a crooked and depraved generation, in which you shine like stars in the universe," one of the men preached.

What did this mean? She tried to make sense of the deepest longings her customers confided to her. They wanted answers from her. Now someone had answers for her. Could she actually be someone's child, not someone's slave?

The stars are not giving me answers? Do answers really come from another god who is not in the stars? Her head was beginning to hurt. This was a powerful change in her thinking. She was struggling with this conflict as she felt the old Spirit of Python start to whisper voices in her mind. She fought the rising confusion by focusing on the vibrant colors in front of her.

Why does the python torment me, just when I am starting to understand a god I cannot see? He is destroying me. She screamed in terror and gripped a stone pedestal while she fought the evil python spirit with all her might, but to no avail. Her vision started to blur; she shook violently. She fell to the ground crumpled up in fetal position. A crowd gathered around and stared.

The paralysis loosened its grip only after the sun had moved from midday to low in the west. Her owners found her in the commotion, and despaired that this time she was lost forever. If she died, then how would they support themselves? They carried her limp body to their house and left her to recover alone while they anxiously wrung their hands and counted coins. A few hours later, with movements like a sleepwalker, she pulled herself up and staggered out of the house back into the marketplace. Again, she was drawn to the crowd around those newcomers, and she listened. The words of the Jewish men rang through her head and she struggled to understand, yet the residue of the seizure fought clarity of thought.

The slave girl repeatedly scrambled to the forefront of any group of people that gathered around the Jewish preachers, to the annoyance of those trying to listen. The short, bald man was Paul. He dressed like one who had not changed robes since the beginning of a long journey. She struggled to stay close enough to him to hear his words, but Paul edged away from her because of her constant hoarse shouting. The crowd followed Paul, and she would be left alone outside of hearing range.

"These men are servants of the Most High God. They are telling you the way to be saved," she incessantly repeated. Her own tired voice struggled to rise out of her throat but could not escape.

"She seems to get the main point," some members of the crowd discussed among themselves. "But the words are coming from the mouth of a demon."

Paul and Silas, the man with him, were directing disturbed looks in her direction. Finally, Paul looked to heaven and seemed to pray; then he walked directly to her and grabbed her by the shoulders. "In the name of Jesus Christ, come out of her."

Her body convulsed. The crowd gasped and strained to witness Paul's action. The sudden silence that fell over the scene offered relief from the constant racket of the marketplace. Meanwhile, the girl collapsed on the cobblestone of the forum in the midst of all the stone idols and shop stalls.

"This girl is our property, and we paid a pot of gold for her," her female owner said, while rushing onto the scene. She almost kicked the prone girl out of the way.

"She was never disturbing anyone. She was not suffering, why did you mess with her? Don't you care about us; how should we live without her? Besides, she practices an allowed Roman cult, which is more than can be said about you Jews. No one else has this kind of talent in Philippi!" her male owner shouted. "If she is dead, I'll have you pay, I'll have you arrested!"

The attention of the whole marketplace was riveted on Paul and the girl's owners. Roman soldiers moved in to break up the fuss. Paul and Silas were led away in handcuffs. The life of a slave girl was not worthy of any attention, except to a woman dressed in purple and her companions who carried the motionless girl away.

FREE OF THE PYTHON'S GRIP

She only knew events of the past few days because her friends later described her erratic and possessed behavior as she regained her strength. Friends—she dreamed with newfound warmth about the people who cared about her—they were the new magic. She had never had friends before! It must have been the next morning, but she really did not know for sure, she had lost all sense of time. She found herself on a cot in a comfortable house. A small group of people surrounded her who seemed to be praying over her.

"Where am I; what has happened? Whatever world I am in, I don't want to leave," the girl mumbled. Her hair had been combed and her face wiped clean.

"She has opened her eyes," a woman softly exclaimed to all those standing around. "Praise be to God. You are going to be okay; you are safe with us."

A pleasant face became clear in front of her eyes. "I am Lydia, and these are my friends, and you are in my house. We have been praying for a miracle, that you would survive."

"I feel like a new person. My mind is clear, and my tongue and mouth are obeying my heart. No longer am I the mouth of the Python. Who is Jesus? I want to jump up and shout with joy!"

"No. No more shouting," the group smiled at each other. "Stay calm."

"What has happened to me? There is so much that I do not understand. Are my owners going to get me?" The girl's questions tumbled out of her mouth.

"A few days ago you started following us all around the city of Philippi wherever Paul and Silas were preaching," they said, filling in the gaps of her memory. "The noise you made was relentless. We were helpless to give you relief, and we are sorry to say that we actually wished you would go away. Your possessed brain caused you to shout out. Your owners retrieved you repeatedly, but you would escape and show up at the fringes of the group and again start the howling."

"Yes, my throat is still sore from the shouting," she said, struggling to explain those horrible days. "I was propelled by my constant tormentor, the python. My body was possessed, and I could not escape the grip of that evil spirit. Then finally, Paul, that man whose words I had been yearning to understand, shouted directly at my face, 'In the name of Jesus Christ, come out of her.'"

"I remember my body shook with one more giant convulsion and suddenly I was overwhelmed by total peace and calm," she continued. "I do not remember anything for a while; I have never been so tired. When I next opened my eyes, it was dark. A sudden tremble woke me up in the dark, and I realized the ground was moving. I was gripped with terror; I thought another convulsion was coming upon me, but it passed quickly."

"There was a short but violent earthquake last night in Philippi," Lydia spoke up. "We checked on you, but you were sleeping like a stone."

"Where are Paul and his companion who were preaching all over the city? He healed me and I must thank him."

"Well, that is another matter for prayer," Lydia continued. "Paul and Silas were taken to prison by the authorities who were trying to break up the near riot that happened when your former owners attacked Paul."

"Paul got in trouble because of me? How horrifying! Instead of thanks for healing me, my owners have caused him to be scourged. I was beginning to feel like a new person, without the huge weight of the past. Now I feel dreadful!" The girl fell back into bed and tears filled her eyes. "And will my owners try to get me back?"

"We paid them some money, which they accepted greedily, because it prevented a complete financial loss for them. They thought you were dead," Lydia continued. "I imagine they have escaped Philippi to stay out of trouble. Now we will see about Paul; we have already seen a huge prayer answered. We will continue to pray."

"I am free of my owners? Do you own me now?" The girl looked at Lydia hopefully.

"Of course not; we do not own other humans. You are a free woman." Lydia nestled her back into bed. "But you are welcome to stay with my household. I can use help with my business."

"Thank you so much. Do I look like a completely new person? I feel new." The former slave girl was discovering the use of her own voice and could not stop. "Now I am who I was meant to be. My mouth is free to speak what I wish, and I do not have to speak lies anymore. It is like a new birth! I am free of the python for the first time in my life. Not only have I gained that freedom, but I am no longer a slave. Wait, I cannot tell fortunes anymore. This may be a new problem."

"There is more to your new birth in Jesus than you can begin to understand right now," Lydia reassured her. "You are only at the beginning of a new journey."

The group smiled at each other with knowing glances. The other members of the household started to tell her wonderful things about real truth, and that she did not have to tell lies anymore.

Suddenly there was a knock at the gate of the courtyard. The girl heard voices through the window, followed by shouts of rejoicing. "Paul is free; Silas is free!"

"You won't believe what happened last night because of the earthquake!" she heard them exclaim in the next room.

"Come in here and tell me. I want to thank you," she urged.

Paul and Silas did not recognize the voice. But upon entering, they could hardly contain their joy. "It is the girl possessed by the spirit of python! Praise God, Lydia found you. Lydia, you are a blessing to so many Christ-followers." Paul turned again to the girl. "I am sorry we lost contact with you yesterday. Immediately after the spirit was expelled, we had our hands full and were taken to jail."

"Yes, that much I was told," she said. "But then what happened last night?"

Everyone gathered close. They were all anxious for the whole story.

"We were thrown into prison," Paul said. He chose not to mention that they had been flogged. "We were placed into the innermost cell of the prison and fastened in stocks."

"Yes, it looked grim for us," Silas added.

"We started singing hymns to God around midnight; after all, what else could we do? The other prisoners were listening," Paul continued.

"Suddenly the earth started shaking," Silas jumped in. "The chains fell lose from our feet; we were suddenly free."

"The prison guard was ready to kill himself, because he was responsible to keep us under guard. The Romans would kill him if he let any prisoners escape. But we all stayed in place and shouted for him to stop. We were all accounted for," Paul exclaimed.

"The jailer fell at our feet and asked how he could be saved." Silas said. The two men were so used to telling stories together, that they talked as one without skipping a beat.

"The jailer took us to his house, cleaned us up, and asked that we baptize him and his family in the name of Jesus," Paul said. "The community of Christ-believers is growing in Philippi. Lydia, you will need a bigger meeting place for all the new believers."

"This morning, the authorities decided we should be released and we were given permission to leave. But we said, 'not so fast, our rights as Roman citizens were violated,'" Silas continued.

"They told us to leave the city quietly, but we are not going quietly, so here we are," Paul said. He had finished the telling of the night's events. "To make the story complete, we find our girl recovering nicely in the caring hands of Lydia. Can you believe all the miracles that have occurred?"

"Actually, I am ready to believe anything is possible with Jesus. I can see into the future, and it looks very bright indeed," said the former slave girl as she sank back into a fluffy down-filled cushion.

My new family . . . what a marvelous word—family . . . that was one meaning of the word freedom, but I have so many freedoms now. I am free of the evil spirit. I am free of my past. I am free of my fear of the future. I am free to speak the message of Jesus to all people who will listen. And now I have the freedom to speak truth and not lies!

The Girl Who Found Her Own Voice

POINTS TO PONDER ABOUT THE GIRL WHO FOUND HER VOICE

This story, our second *Bold Girl* taken from the book of Acts, took place in the Greek city of Philippi, which was an outpost of the huge Roman Empire. Paul was in Philippi during his second missionary journey. He had traveled for the first time into the continent of Europe, as the result of a dream (Acts 16:9–10). The Holy Spirit called Paul to move away from Palestine, the center of this new movement of Christ-followers, into new territory. Be sure to read the New Testament text from Acts 16:11–40 to determine the parts of this *Bold Girls* story that are directly from the Bible and the parts that are fictional additions. Do you think the fictional parts are realistic to what this girl may have experienced?

This story has many characteristics in common with the other *Bold Girls* stories. First, the main character is again a servant girl, and she is also unnamed. Second, this story is about a girl who uses her voice. It is interesting when one considers that in many traditions, women, and especially children, are supposed to be seen but not heard. But the girls in these stories use their voices and are heard!

At the beginning of this story, our girl had a voice, but it was not her own. Something very strange and hard for us to understand is described in the Bible passage about her. The girl was possessed by an evil spirit. Several texts in the Bible describe people who are possessed by the devil. In the times of Jesus and the apostles after him, this was something that did occur. This condition is recorded numerous times in the New Testament.

The experts in Bible study do not always agree about how to interpret phenomena such as this. It will take some time, study, and discussion for you to begin to understand it. Some commentaries will explain that "possession" is how people in ancient times understood mental illnesses and seizure disorders. Today, we know these are medical conditions that are caused by physical abnormalities in the brain.

Nevertheless, consider that something more is going on in this story. The state of being possessed by an evil spirit or a devil really was a condition that occurred at that time, and still occurs today nearer than we may imagine. These phenomena occurred to demonstrate the power of Jesus, and the apostles after him. They were able to destroy evil in the world, whether it was sickness, natural disasters, death, or evil spirits. Whether we are afflicted with an illness or the possession by an evil spirit, the message is that Jesus came into this world to heal.

Bold Girls Speak

Try to imagine a girl completely incapable of acting and talking the way she wants to. She is a slave, both physically, as a human owned by another human, and mentally because an evil spirit controlled her. Something or someone inhabits her body and controls everything she says and does. As a slave, she is owned by people who exploit her awful condition in order to earn money. The book of Acts notes that she is bringing in much money by telling fortunes for her masters. The story unfolds when Paul comes to Philippi. The poor girl follows Paul and his partner Silas everywhere they go.

"These men are bond servants of the Most High God, who are proclaiming to you the way of salvation," she shouts out. This is puzzling, because it sounds like she is telling the truth. Since it seems she was declaring the truth about Paul and Silas, why then did they need to heal her? She was, after all, attracting a lot of attention to them! Even if the message was technically correct, it was not coming from her. The devil was controlling her thoughts and words, and not the Spirit of God. Sometimes, even today, people talk about God and what they say may sound very logical, but God is not in their heart and not controlling their words.

Finally, Paul cannot tolerate the disturbance anymore. "I command you in the name of Jesus Christ to come out of her!" The spirit immediately left the girl. She was completely healed. When such an evil possession occurred, it provided an opportunity for a miracle to be performed. Miracles then and today serve the purpose of showing the power of God to heal. It is God's will that people are well and not ill. Jesus, Paul, and others, performed miracles of healing, and some of those involved "casting out devils," such as in this case.

What a relief for this girl! Now she can proclaim Christ and speak with her own voice. What happened to her immediately after the miracle of her healing? According to this fictional *Bold Girls* story, she has a happy future, but the actual Bible passage gives us no hint of what happened to her. How would you have imagined her future?

This *Bold Girls* story is only one possible scenario. We do not know how her new life progressed. Acts 16:13–15 describes a community in Philippi that met to pray by the river, led by a woman named Lydia. Paul and the others in his party stayed at her house. Lydia would no doubt have known the events connected with Paul that occurred in Philippi, especially since he was her houseguest. It was an amazing time for Lydia as well, because Paul baptized her and her household in the name of Jesus (Acts 16:15). Lydia is an interesting woman in her own right, and she was an early leader of the young Christian church in Philippi. It is not unreasonable to

The Girl Who Found Her Own Voice

imagine that the story of this *Bold Girl* came to a happy ending when they found each other. How the life of this slave girl proceeded from the point of her healing remains as much of a mystery to us as her name. Like many unnamed people in the Bible who have been often overlooked, this girl surely used her new voice to tell her story about her new freedom in Jesus.

QUESTIONS FOR DISCUSSION

1. Can healing miracles occur today? What counts as a miracle? Do miracles of any kind happen today? Can you think of examples?

2. Do you think this girl at Philippi had a mental illness or some kind of evil spirit-induced madness? What difference does this make in how we understand the power of Jesus? Jesus heals all kinds of illness, but this story also shows us that he has power over the evil of the world.

3. Read the whole story of Paul and Silas and how they escaped from prison. Later in the story, when Paul and Silas are released from prison by means of an earthquake, they baptize the jailer (and his family) who was in great fear of being punished for letting the prisoners escape. This situation is similar to the story of Peter (Acts 12:5–17) where he was released from prison by an angel. But in that story the guards who were responsible for guarding Peter were executed. What is God showing in these two accounts of prison guards?

4. In the letter to the Philippians, Paul mentions several believers by name. The group in Philippi prospered economically enough to share money with Paul. What was Lydia's business?

RELATED CULTURAL AND HISTORICAL QUESTIONS TO EXPLORE

1. Read John 9:1–3. Why are some people born with disabilities? How should we treat people born with special challenges? How can we help them? What did Jesus do?

2. Are you interested in horoscopes, fortune telling, Ouija boards, Tarot cards, and other ways of telling the future? Do they work? Are they a good way to plan your future? Could these techniques be a dangerous influence, or are they innocent fun if they are not taken seriously?

SUGGESTED TOPICS OF DISCUSSION FOR TEACHERS AND PARENTS OF OLDER STUDENTS

1. The *Bold Girls* story of Miriam, from the book of Exodus, also involves slavery. During the time of Miriam, the whole nation of Israel was in slavery. Namaan's servant girl, from the book of 2 Kings, was also a slave. And most certainly, the girl in this story was a slave. How widespread is slavery today? Discuss the atrocities of human trafficking. What stance does the Bible take toward slavery? Historically, how has the church handled this issue?

2. The dangers and attractions of fortune-telling can be further discussed. What fortune-telling devices are available today and where are these skills practiced? What kind of knowledge do people seek by consulting fortune-tellers? Where should Christians look for guidance and advice about the future?

3. The possibility that a person can be possessed by an evil spirit now in modern times is a matter of much controversy and is certainly not to be taken lightly. Remember you do not have to have answers to difficult issues immediately; many questions we struggle with our entire lives.

The Daughters Who Prophesied

ACTS 21:8–35

RACHEL

"Take care! Try to pick out Paul before the others notice him. He is expected within the week, so keep a sharp lookout." Rachel scanned the harbor for new ships that arrived during the night. The rising sun reflecting off the lighthouse of Caesarea caused her to squint in her search for the grain clipper from Ptolemais that could be carrying the beloved passengers. Her father, Philip, had emphasized the errand's importance. "Check the waterfront first thing every morning, but don't attract attention by asking strangers for news of recent arrivals."

The imposing temple of Roma and Augustus, built of gleaming white marble, cast a long, cold shadow over the harbor. This powerful reminder of Roman rule and pagan gods dominated the city and was impossible to ignore. Rachel, as the youngest of four daughters, was assigned the task of walking up and down the docks until the sun was higher in the sky and the morning chill had burned off. She hoped that nothing had happened to them at sea. Paul, Luke, and seven others in the group should be arriving any day. As soon as they set foot upon the dock, she would discreetly direct them to her house, where she lived with three older sisters and her father.

The great Apostle Paul's life was under dire threat. Strict observers of Jewish law were desperate to see him dead, because he dared to preach to non-Jews, or Gentiles. The Christ-followers were certain he would be arrested, and then his execution could follow! Paul was a man either much loved, or much hated, since his miraculous encounter with the risen Christ about twenty-five years ago. At that time, her father had been one of a group of seven Greek-speaking men who had chosen to serve the Greek

Christians of Jerusalem. Among them was a man called Stephen. Rachel inhaled sharply. The tragic story her father told of his friend, Stephen, made her shudder. But after his martyrdom, the gospel news had spread rapidly.

She quickened her step, dodging the fish merchants while studying every face of the new arrivals. Paul was now quite elderly. His formerly athletic body now stooped and his head bald. His prominent nose and heavy eyebrows would be the same as in his younger years. Luke was a younger man; that much she knew. She did not know anything about the other men. Her father was well known in the city and did not wish to endanger Paul by being seen with him. Caesarea was the seaport closest to Jerusalem, and fast enough news of his arrival reach his enemies.

Her feet seemed self-guided to a particular dock. Coming toward her, staggering down a gangplank with unsteady legs, were some sea-weary men. They looked around for a familiar face. Although Rachel spoke Greek, like the majority of the city population, she also knew a few Hebrew phrases. She sought the gaze of the obvious group leader and spoke softly to him.

"How did you pick us out of the crowd?" Paul asked. He seemed to be puzzled by the greeting in Hebrew and her ability to find him so efficiently.

"I'm one of Philip's daughters," she replied. She felt as though they were able to read each other's minds. "He told me to be on the lookout for you. Come with me. I'll show you the way to our home."

HELEN

"Just a few weeks ago I was further north on the coast in the city of Troas," Paul said. We sat spellbound in our house, listening to the latest news of Paul's travels. "I know I get carried away with preaching too long sometimes, but I was leaving the next day. A young man named Eutychus listened to me while seated on a windowsill. Well, I admit many lamps overheated the room; he dozed off and fell out of a third floor window while I was talking. He hit the ground hard. We feared that he had perished."

We gasped in horror. "What happened; how is he?" I quickly asked. Paul looked startled that I had interrupted his story. He glanced at my father.

"Oh, this is my second youngest daughter, Helen," my father quickly introduced me. "I encourage my daughters to ask plenty of questions." Paul smiled, not the least offended.

The Daughters Who Prophesied

"The young people should ask plenty of questions," Paul added, but then he hesitated to continue telling the story. He seemed to be thinking about the young man fatally injured. "You know I have a nephew in Jerusalem that age," he said softly.

Luke continued the story when Paul fell silent. Paul is still blessed with miraculous healing powers. We all rushed down to Eutychus. Paul threw himself on top of him and clasped his arms around him. Eutychus drew breath again. We were all so relieved; we broke bread, ate, and Paul continued preaching until daylight."

"Luke, have you written this down?" I asked. "That story is new to us." We were riveted by the adventures of Paul and Luke, which included not only harrowing stories of persecution but also stories of miracles and many new believers. We already knew of Paul's adventures through his letters that were regularly delivered to our house. But to hear them retold in his own voice made us think we were actually there. My sisters and I copied and then sent his letters on to other believers, so that Paul's teachings about Christ's saving work would be spread as quickly as possible. Although it was unusual that girls could read and write, our father saw to it that we were educated. We were also riveted by the discussions of many people who came to our house from many countries, even Africa.

A few days later our nine visitors looked much fresher and at ease. Many of the Christ-followers in Caesarea had joined us that evening. The night grew late as Paul told of yet another narrow escape from a riot in Ephesus. Wherever Paul goes, turbulence follows. We shivered at the stories of many miraculous escapes he had endured.

Recently arrived from Judea, Agabus, a well-known prophet, suddenly jumped to his feet in the middle of our small group.

"What are you doing?" I asked, startled.

Agabus seemed intent on disrobing Paul by removing the sash from around his waist. Several small items fell out and clattered to the tile floor including a bag of coins. "Here, tie my hands together with Paul's belt," Agabus said, extending his hands to me. I did as he asked, because I was too shocked to protest.

Agabus assumed a kneeling posture and words came out of his mouth that did not sound like his voice, "This is the word of the Holy Spirit! In this way, the Jews at Jerusalem will bind the man who owns this belt and deliver him into the hands of the Romans."

The Christ-followers with us began to cry and plead with Paul to remain in Caesarea. Rachel and I glanced at each other, and then at our older sisters.

"Is this what prophecy sounds like?" I whispered to Rachel under the protests and wailing of the crowd. The local group of Christ-followers knew our two older sisters as prophets, but we had never seen our sisters talk like Agabus had in the assembly. It was rumored that we would also be prophets. How would we know?

"If this is prophecy, then he is not saying anything new. Paul already knows he is in danger if he goes to Jerusalem," Susanne, our oldest sister whispered back. "He just doesn't know the details of how it will happen. Agabus says that the Jews will seize Paul, tie him up, and turn him over to the Romans."

"If he is really speaking as a prophet, then his words should be true," I added.

"Apparently we know something the others don't," Suzanne observed.

"Agabus will not discourage Paul from going to Jerusalem. Paul already knows he will probably face prison and perhaps death," said Gaby, our second oldest sister, who is very insightful.

The Daughters Who Prophesied

"What are you doing, weeping and breaking my heart? For I am ready not only to be bound, but even to die in Jerusalem for the name of the Lord Jesus," Paul pleaded with the audience and Agabus.

We recalled how several months ago, according to one of his letters, Paul changed his plans to return to Caesarea by sea because of rumors of danger from those who could put his ship into peril. He left more than a few enemies in Ephesus when, because of Paul's conversions of Christ-believers, the silversmiths lost their income from making silver idols and rioted in protest. In addition, Paul was intent on bringing a large contribution of money for the Christians of Jerusalem.

"Yes, I soon must move on to Jerusalem. The relaxation and fellowship here at the house of Philip and his daughters is my piece of heaven on earth, but I have more roads ahead. If, God willing, I survive Jerusalem, I am going on to Rome," Paul explained.

My sisters and I could only say, "The will of the Lord be done!"

We knew that no amount of tears and pleading would change Paul's mind. Agabus had been right in the past; he predicted a famine around Jerusalem several years ago, which is the reason for the gift of money to the Jerusalem Christians. This time, he just stated the obvious, repeating what was already well known.

What Agabus did not know was that Paul's upcoming arrest in Jerusalem would not be his last. Paul would survive to go on to Rome, I was sure of this. That was his plan, and I believed it would come to pass.

Then as now, the Spirit speaks to all who listen!

RACHEL

The joyous days passed and soon Paul informed our family that he was ready to make the two-day journey to Jerusalem. "Father please, may Helen and I go along with Paul and the others to Jerusalem?" we asked. We had been there before, but never without our older sisters or father.

"The girls can stay with my sister's family in Jerusalem," Paul reassured my father. "My sister has a son about their age. I will look out for them."

"We may need to look out for Paul," I, the youngest said. Paul just grinned at me.

"The younger generation needs to have firsthand experience with the issues," Father added. "They can report back to me what happens." Father was well aware of the dangers that faced Paul, but he was also convinced that Paul would go on to Rome.

"Yes, let the girls go," our oldest sisters reassured Father. "Susanne and I will stay in Caesarea to look after things." Since the death of our mother, our older sisters ran the busy household of Philip. Our father was often gone for extended journeys to evangelize in the Gentile areas of Samaria and the coastline.

We were very excited to leave for Jerusalem in a small caravan with Paul, Luke, and their companions on pack animals. Paul continued to face the future with joy in Jesus. We sensed the guiding of the most Powerful One who was going to see Paul to Rome, one way or the other. We were confident that whatever happened in Jerusalem would only be a detour.

Upon reaching the city, Paul guided us through the maze of narrow streets. "Here is the street where my sister lives. My nephew knows every nook and cranny of Jerusalem," Paul told us. He rang the bell at a gate. He greeted his sister and nephew with kisses and introduced us. "This is my nephew, Joseph." We quickly felt at home.

"See you in the morning; we are looking forward to exploring Jerusalem," we said before we headed to our sleeping room.

At first daylight, we were happily underway throughout the streets of Jerusalem. The diversity of visitors in the city at Pentecost was amazing, but we could also feel the tension of so many people together in tight spaces.

"The constant conflicts are based on our differences: Gentiles against Jews; Christian Gentiles versus Christian Jews, and Christ-believers and the traditional Jews, not to mention plenty of disagreements between various Jews themselves," explained Joseph.

"We have enough experience in Caesarea with the Roman government that mistrusts everyone," Helen added. "Their only interest is to maintain peace, and crush rebellions before they start so Rome does not have to get involved."

"What is it about differences between us that cause so much difficulty?" I asked.

"For instance, consider our differences. You are girls and I am a boy," Joseph smiled at us hopefully. Helen and I glanced at each other—*So he just now noticed?*

"All right, thanks for pointing that out," I teased. "We are very glad your Greek is better than our Aramaic. We know very little Aramaic or Hebrew. Our ancestors left Judea many generations ago, gave up speaking

Aramaic, and picked up Greek customs because Jerusalem and the temple were far away. Our parents were Christ-followers from the very earliest days, even before Paul 'saw the light.' We were baptized as infants."

Joseph then recounted his history. "My mother grew up with Paul and received the strictest Jewish education in all the Jewish laws and Hebrew. "She became a Christ-believer when Uncle Paul began preaching, and he baptized me when I was older. As Jewish Christians we still follow all the Jewish customs such as temple sacrifices, holidays, and circumcision, but we believe in Jesus as the Messiah."

My sister and I gulped at the mention of circumcision, which we had certainly read about many times in Paul's letters, but it was not a topic of daily conversation in a household of girls.

"We, too, believe in Jesus as the Messiah and Redeemer, which your uncle has explained," I recovered, trying to redirect the conversation.

"Yes, indeed, I haven't had much contact with him, but in Jerusalem we receive copies of his letters," Joseph explained.

"In fact, we have copied many of those letters. You may have read some of our handwriting in Greek," Helen quickly added.

"Really? You write a good script, and no wonder you know my uncle so well," Joseph said. He looked at us with new respect.

"I think the death of Stephen and his persecution of many other men and women weighs heavily upon Paul. He has recklessly abandoned his own health and safety for many years to make amends, although he knows this is never possible. Only in Jesus are even our worst sins forgiven," I said.

"I know that your father, Philip, was with Stephen in the early days," said Joseph. "He has courageously witnessed in Samaria and now there are believers as far away as Africa because of his encounter with the Ethiopian eunuch. Did he ever talk to you about being miraculously whisked away by the Holy Spirit?" Joseph asked.

"No, he is strangely silent about that; our father was a young man in those years. After that he traveled down the coast to Caesarea and settled there when he met our mother," Rachel said. "I will try again to get him to open up about that unusual flight."

"This history must not be forgotten. More important events are yet to come and we will be part of them," Joseph observed. Then he quickly glanced around. "Have you been watching the way through these narrow streets? I think we are lost."

HELEN

Rachael and I somehow always made it back to Joseph's house and learned our way around the streets of Jerusalem. Joseph greeted us one morning: "I want you to meet someone very important. Paul is going to see James this morning, the half brother of Jesus. He is quite elderly, but still the leader of the Jerusalem assembly. Let's go see what is going on," Joseph urged.

"We will see someone who was close to Jesus," Rachael said. She was excited. All of us were excited.

We walked through winding alleys, under arches, and across plazas with shops. This was a city much different from Caesarea, which is laid out in straight streets, Roman style. We opened heavy doors to a synagogue and crowded into the back. James, Paul, and other elders were standing in the middle of the long rows facing a middle aisle, already in animated conversation. Paul had just presented a considerable gift of money to James for the Jerusalem believers. This should have been a joyous occasion of solidarity between the Jerusalem Christians and Gentile Christians, but the receipt of this gift provoked only lukewarm response.

"What happened to the celebration we all anticipated?" I asked

"If the Jewish Christians accept the money, then it appears that they approve the teachings of Paul, but he seems to be saying that the laws of Torah do not apply anymore," Joseph tried to explain.

"As Greek Christians, we do not follow the Torah laws, isn't that okay?" Rachel asked.

"If I understand my uncle correctly, Paul allows Jewish Christians to continue their Jewish ways, but Gentile Christians are not required to keep Torah laws," Joseph explained.

"Do the Jewish Christians want everyone to keep the Jewish law?" I questioned.

"Yes, in the case of circumcision that is particularly difficult." There, he said the word again. I tried to think of a way to change the subject, but Joseph quickly continued. "Since the Jerusalem council ten years ago, Gentile Christians are only required not to eat blood, strangled animals, or food offered to sacrifices, and not to engage in sexual sins," Joseph said. He had no qualms talking about anything.

I quietly nudged Rachel, "Maybe because we do not have brothers, we just are not used to the way boys talk."

"Remember, we have copied Paul's letters, and the letters to the Galatians and Corinthians cover these topics," I said, deftly changing the subject.

"But it is one thing to copy words, and another to see the outcomes carried out here in Jerusalem."

"Yes, in the letter to the Galatians Paul has some choice things to say about those who insist on circumcision for new converts who are Gentiles," now Rachel had said the word.

"Uncle Paul doesn't mince words," Joseph grinned. "I guess I resemble him in that way. And yes, I am not around girls very much. Some of the elders will be scandalized that we are seen together in the streets, but I could get used to the Hellenistic custom of men and women mingling more."

"It appears that James is trying to come up with a solution," I noted. We turned our attention to the proceedings in the synagogue, but I struggled with the language.

"He is suggesting that Paul carry out a special vow of the Jewish law as read in the Torah," Joseph said, doing his best to translate the Aramaic for us. "Paul has agreed to not drink any wine, not cut his hair or beard, and keep himself ceremonially clean for seven days to show his dedication to God."

"But what does this accomplish for Paul," I asked.

"This will show that Paul does not object to the Torah requirements for Jewish Christians, and they have nothing to fear from him. According to this purification rite, Paul must return to the Temple on the eighth day," Joseph said. He was well informed on the Torah.

"Is it possible that his enemies will be planning to ambush him since they know when he will be in the Temple?" I asked while trying to deny the shiver of fear that came over me.

"Not only do I know a lot about your father, but your two older sisters are known as prophetesses. Do you practice prophecy also?" Joseph asked.

"Two prophetesses in the family create enough events in our house, along with our famous father. We try to follow the lead of the Spirit, but we are not looking to be called prophets," Rachel said without conviction. I think my sister was also beginning to see events line up into an unstoppable tragedy, and trying to recover.

RACHAEL

We spent the next week exploring Jerusalem; we climbed on the walls and visited the market places. These sunny days would have been among the most pleasant of my life, had it not been for the deep shadows that came over me whenever I thought of Paul. As Pentecost came nearer, the crowds increased. Joseph showed us sites where events of Jesus' last days of life on earth took place about thirty years ago. Eerily, it could seem that Paul was following the same path, but I did not think so. I was certain he would survive Jerusalem and go to Rome.

"Paul left a lot of enemies in Ephesus. I hope they don't come here and stir things up," Joseph said. "We must listen to the echoes in the streets. Because we are young, people do not pay attention to us. Today Paul goes to the Temple for the purification rite, and I am going in as well. I am a circumcised Jewish male, and I am permitted to go into the Court of the Israelites."

"That is definitely more information than we need," I said. Both Helen and I turned red. "We do not care to go through the purification rites necessary to enter the Temple; besides; we could not even get into the Women's Court. We are not Jewish anymore," my sister and I agreed. We entered the Hulda Gate in the south wall and climbed up covered stairs to reach the platform. "We will wait for you at this entrance," Helen called back to Joseph as we parted company.

The whole Temple Mount was crowded with worshipers. We moved forward until we stood not far from a sign that clearly warned us, in Latin and Greek, not to go any farther: "Gentiles do not proceed past this gate or your death is your own responsibility."

"No chance of misunderstanding that. We will stand our ground here in front of the gate. Paul must pass through to get into the inner courts," I said. We did not have to wait long. All heads turned toward him as though he was someone famous, which in a way, he was.

"There he is," said Helen. She is a little taller than me. "He has four other men with him, apparently the other Jews he supported in the purification rite. Such a crowd is pressing around him; it is hard to tell who is with him." A buzz passed from person to person, and soon there was jostling and shouting. We feared a riot was in the making, and we were retreating to the entrance when we saw Paul being attacked by the mob.

"What are they doing to Paul?" I shouted to Helen. We stopped in our tracks as the dreadful scene unfolded. "Men are holding his arms behind him and others are pounding him with their fists," I said. We stood frozen at the sight. He was helpless to fend off the blows.

"How could this be happening? What did he do?" Helen sobbed.

"He was in the process of carrying out prescribed Jewish purity laws," I said, my voice rising. "Stop it! . . . What are you doing to an innocent man?"

Helen also shouted at the top of her lungs. We were hardly heard over the noise, but a few people glanced in our direction.

"We have to help Paul; where is Joseph?" I screamed.

Above the noise of the crowd, clashes of heavy doors slamming shut bounced off the walls. The courts of the Temple were now locked, leaving many people trapped inside. We tried to push our way toward Paul to help him, as though we could actually make a difference. We were almost run over by armored Roman soldiers who tramped in from the nearby Antonia Fortress. The crowd fell away from Paul at the sight of Roman swords and shields, and he was left exposed as a crumpled heap on the stone floor. Soldiers lifted him to his feet. We were relieved to see him standing on his own; at least he was not dead. Then the commander chained each of Paul's hands to a soldier.

"According to Agabus's prophecy, it was the Jews who were supposed to tie up Paul, not the Romans," Helen remembered.

"Who are you and what have you done?" we heard the commander ask Paul.

But we did not hear Paul's answer. His voice was drowned out by the roar of the raging crowd. "Get rid of him! Rid the earth of him! He is not fit to live!"

The soldiers forced Paul in the direction of the barracks where steps led up to a door. Then we saw Paul hold up his hands. We held our breaths. The noise level of the crowd dropped to a murmur and Paul began to speak in Aramaic:

"I am a Jew, born in Tarsus of Cilicia, but brought up in this city. I studied under Gamaliel, and I was thoroughly trained in the law of our ancestors." Paul continued to tell his life story as a Jew who encountered Jesus on the road to Damascus. The crowd remained very quiet through his lengthy speech until he said, "Then the Lord said to me, 'Go; I will send you far away to the Gentiles.'"

A riot exploded with terrifying shouting and shoving.

The Roman commander persisted in trying to get Paul to confess to something. Because Paul denied any wrongdoing, they tied him up to be flogged in order to extract a confession. At the raising of a whip, we squeezed our eyes shut. Neither could we move forward or backward.

"Is it legal for you to flog a Roman citizen who hasn't even been found guilty?" Paul asked, finally saying something in his own defense. The whip was lowered and we dared to breathe.

"Tell me, are you a Roman citizen?" The commander fell back and froze.

"Yes, I am," Paul answered. "I was born a citizen." Then the Roman soldiers released him from the chains. Several men hoisted him to their shoulders and carried him into the barracks for safekeeping from the fury of the crowd.

After Paul was out of sight, the crowd started to stream out of the Temple area. We returned to our present reality and frantically looked for Joseph. But he was nowhere to be found. We had to give up looking for him and made our way back to Joseph's house. His mother was nearly faint with fear about her brother, as well as her son, when we told her about the events.

"It is easier when Paul is far away and I don't know about his daily dangers," Paul's sister moaned. Suddenly, Joseph entered the door. He was out of breath from running. We all greeted him with tears of thankfulness.

"I was locked in the Court of the Israelites when the Temple guards shut the doors. I did not see what happened to Paul; tell me about it," Joseph implored. He was impatient with curiosity, and we described the chaos as best we could.

"Paul may not even be safe in the Antonia Barracks. I heard fearful comments while I was locked in the Temple. Some strict Jews from Ephesus were exclaiming how they hated him. I hunkered down to not be recognized," Joseph said, telling of his experience.

"How can they hate Paul so much?" I asked.

"They talked about forming a conspiracy to kill Paul, and they will not eat or drink until Paul was dead," Joseph continued. Paul's sister gasped at hearing this news.

"Tonight, at least, he should be safe in the barracks," Joseph said. "We will see what tomorrow brings. May the Lord bring him rest tonight."

"We know he will go to Rome; we know it as though we are prophets," I said. "Let us pray that God keeps him safe."

The Daughters Who Prophesied

HELEN

Later the next day we learned that Paul had already appeared before the Sanhedrin, the rulers of the Jews. That did not go well. "God will strike you, you whitewashed wall! You sit there to judge me according to the law, yet you yourself violate the law by commanding that I be struck!" Paul boldly proclaimed.

We agreed that sounded like Paul; he continued to speak his mind.

"What was he talking about?" I was confused.

"Well, he is talking about . . . whitewashed walls . . . maybe white and clean on the outside, but rotten on the inside. I admit, I don't know either," Joseph said. He was at a loss for a full explanation. "But, I imagine the members of the Sanhedrin were not flattered by the comparison." Joseph continued to describe what he had heard. "Yet, some of the Pharisees believed him and said, 'We find nothing wrong with this man; what if a spirit or an angel has spoken to him?'"

"At least he has some allies," Paul's sister said, finding some consolation. "We must reach Paul in prison. I am sure he needs food and medical attention, which his friends and family need to provide for him."

"Tomorrow we will find Paul, but how will we get the guards to let us in? They are not likely to regard us with much respect as youngsters, and on top of that they will never pay attention to mere girls," I added. "We must think of a way to help him and find out more about this plan to kill him."

The next morning Joseph's mother had a basket filled with food ready to be taken to her brother. "Go to the guards," she told Joseph, Rachel, and me. "Remind them that Paul is a Roman citizen, and that you are yourself the grandson of a citizen."

"We will find a way. Paul will be safe," I added.

"So it is your skill at prophecy again," Joseph observed. "I will be officially a Roman citizen at age fourteen. I am not much short of that, it will have to work," Joseph said. "Well, let us set out with the supplies."

As we soon discovered, the Antonia Fortress was a huge complex that guarded the north side of the Temple Mount. The building served several purposes. It had apartments for visiting royalty, quarters for Roman soldiers, and a prison, where we knew Paul was being kept.

"How will we get in?" We looked up at the massive walls and only felt discouragement; Roman guards mulled around. We three paused at the moat and stared into the water, each of us sunken in our silent prayers. Several minutes passed.

"I know who you are," a voice whispered behind us. We glanced around to see a huge Roman soldier looming behind us. "You are the nephew of Paul and the daughters of Philip. You are followers of the Way." We felt doomed. "Go to shop number XXXIII in the bazaar if you want to help Paul," he told us. Then he was gone.

"Did you hear that?" I asked.

"Is this a trap?" Rachel asked.

"Does he know Paul?" I asked. "How does he know us?"

"We have no choice but to trust the information from the soldier," Joseph said. "I can find the shop." We wandered deep into the bazaar past many colorful stalls, each with its own products to sell.

"There is XXXIII. Let's just casually go up to the vendor and pretend interest in his wares," Joseph suggested. "He sells metal objects, and he also is dressed like a Pharisee. This could be good or bad."

"Hello, sir. Yes, I do like your inkwells," Helen said to the seller, who noticed her interest. She did not have to pretend expertise in writing materials.

"Young lady, do you write?" he asked.

"Yes, I do. This inkwell is particularly nice for mixing lampblack and oil to form ink," Helen said. While she engaged him, I eyed other objects in the shop and nudged Joseph.

The shopkeeper then turned his attention to me. "Are you interested in that fish-shaped metal plaque? Notice the Greek letters, ΙΧΘΥΣ. Can you read them?"

I turned the rather heavy object in my hand. "Of course I can read the Greek letters," I ventured, but I did not know if I should let him know everything I knew. They were the initials that stood for "Jesus Christ, Son of God Savior." I had to know if I could trust him. If he knew what the letters meant, then I could be sure he was a Christ-follower.

"It means *Iesous Christos, Theos Yios Soter*," the merchant informed me, as though he was telling me something new. "If you bought this, you could nail it to the back of your chariot." The merchant winked.

"I will purchase one as a souvenir for my father; he has a chariot. We will also buy an inkwell; what is your price?" I asked as I got out my coin purse.

"I know who you are. You are followers of the Way," the merchant repeated the phrase we heard earlier. My hands paused in fear as he continued

The Daughters Who Prophesied

to speak. "I am glad to see you, the daughters of Philip and the nephew of Paul."

"How do you know? . . ." I started to stammer.

"Could you recognize the Roman soldier again who told you to come here?" the merchant asked. "Go back to the Antonia Fortress and look for that soldier when he is standing guard. He will let you in. Paul has been witnessing to his Roman guards. This one has become a Christ-follower. Warn Paul that there is a plot by the Sanhedrin to get him out of the prison on the pretense that they need to question him more. He must not leave the safety of the prison for any reason. They will ambush him and kill him."

We quickly made our way back to the Antonia somewhat mystified, but much more confident. We looked for the big Roman soldier and sure enough, he was now standing guard.

"If all three of us go in, it will attract attention since several people seem to have noticed we are together," Helen noted. "I think we need to let Joseph approach the soldier and go in alone. Is that all right with you, Joseph?"

"Yes, I agree I need to be the one to go in since I am a close relative to Paul," Joseph agreed.

"And don't forget that you are almost a Roman citizen," I added with an encouraging hug. "We are with you in prayers; we will meet you at your house."

"Be sure to remember everything to tell us later," Helen added.

Fortunately, we knew the winding streets that led the way back to his house. Joseph's mother eagerly heard everything we experienced. We waited and prayed, but Joseph did not come back. By evening the sky became darkly foreboding, and we still did not hear from him.

"Dear Jesus, please keep Paul and Joseph safe," I prayed. "Please pave the way for Paul to go to Rome and continue his preaching."

We could not sleep, so we did not go to bed; we tried not to imagine the worst. Close to midnight, a clattering at the outside gate woke us from half sleep. We jumped up to see Joseph falling through the house door.

"Hurry, pack up!" Joseph shouted to us. Then he told his mother, "Helen and Rachel are going back to Caesarea with Paul, Luke, and the rest of his group."

We gasped with joy.

"Paul is safe. Joseph is safe. Praise God!" I shouted, and then scrambled to gather our things to travel.

"Mother, can I go, too? We will be riding with Roman soldiers," Joseph pleaded. "Paul must get out of Jerusalem immediately to avoid those who want to kill him. He is still a prisoner, but he will be tried in Caesarea."

"Yes, he certainly can stay at our house," I added.

We threw everything into our bags. In no time, a couple Roman horses were outside our door with the big Roman soldier we saw earlier. It was like a dream; we each got on a splendid horse with a soldier, soon joined the rest of the group with Paul and Luke, and rode like the wind back to Caesarea.

The next day we were at home, and we retold everything to our father and sisters.

"Daughters of Philip, I will have recorded, for all to remember, your marvelous skills in prophecy and your deeds in promoting the saving work of Jesus," Paul told us during the first of many visits we made to the prison of the royal palace of Caesarea where he was being held. "Luke is writing everything on papyrus sheets. A plot to kill me was diverted by the good work of Joseph and you, Helen, and Rachel. If the Sanhedrin had managed to get me out of the prison, then I do not want to imagine what would have happened. All of this was for my safety. I rarely have had the privilege of riding with such splendid horses and guards." Paul chuckled at the memory. "I will request a hearing before Caesar himself, and my dream of going to Rome will come true! May the daughters of Philip and my nephew in Jerusalem continue their work for the message of Christ. On the day of Pentecost, about thirty years ago, Peter predicted that "both sons and daughters would prophecy." The future for the followers of the Way looks bright indeed."

The Daughters Who Prophesied

POINTS TO PONDER ABOUT THE DAUGHTERS WHO PROPHESIED

> Acts 21:8–9: And on the next day we departed and came to Caesarea; and entering the house of Philip the evangelist, who was one of the seven, we stayed with him. Now this man had four virgin daughters who were prophetesses.

> Acts 23:16: But the son of Paul's sister heard of their ambush, and he came and entered the barracks and told Paul.

Have you ever heard of these daughters? You are not alone if you have not. Hardly any mention is made of them in Bible story collections and commentaries, although their father, Philip the Evangelist, is well known. These girls were remarkable enough to be mentioned by Luke in the book of Acts, which he wrote to chronicle Paul's activities.

Prophecy is a gift that raises many more questions than can be easily answered. It is very difficult to discern exactly what the gift of prophecy means, either in the first century or in our present day. Many men in the Old Testament were known as prophets, as were some women. These women prophets include Miriam, Hulda, and Deborah in the Old Testament, and Anna in the beginning of the New Testament times. These women were prophets in the sense that they were able to determine events that would happen in the future.

What can be determined from the Bible about the gift of prophecy? In 1 Corinthians 14:3, a prophet is described as "one who prophesies speaks to people for edification and exhortation and consolation." In other words, a prophet is a person who has a special ability in spiritual discernment and interpretation; that is, preaching and teaching. A common explanation of prophecy is the gift of foretelling, and also "forth-telling," or the proclamation of God's word.

In Acts 2:17 Peter is preaching at the event of the first Pentecost. "And it shall be in the last days, God says, that I will pour forth of my spirit upon all humankind: and your sons and your daughters shall prophesy, and your young men shall see visions." Prophecy is a spiritual gift mentioned along with many other gifts. According to 1 Corinthians 12:28: "And God has appointed in the church, first apostles, second prophets, third teachers, then miracles, then gifts of healings, helps, administrations, and various kinds of tongues." In verse 31 of the same chapter, it is stated that believers are to seek the "higher gifts." Note that there are never any restrictions as to gender whenever spiritual gifts are mentioned in the Bible. From 1 Corinthians 11:5, we know that women prophesied in the public meetings of the early Christians. Paul's only concern about what must have been a routine occurrence is that the women, while prophesying, were appropriately dressed according to the cultural norm.

Philip's daughters, as portrayed in Acts 21:9, had the natural God-given abilities of keen intelligence, curiosity, and courage. Equally important, their father nurtured and encouraged their gifts. In this fictional *Bold Girls* account, the two younger daughters are the main characters who are searching to find their calling in the service of the kingdom. They are not sure they have this gift of prophecy as their older sisters do. Like these young *Bold Girls*, young readers of these biblical stories are probably also struggling to determine where their gifts lie and what their future professions will be.

What an amazing father these *Bold Girls* had! We can safely derive his nature from the few words of the biblical text we have about Philip. He acknowledged the gifts of his daughters, and he did not hinder the work of the Spirit. He did not indicate that prophecy was inappropriate for women. Nothing in the biblical account of Philip's daughters mentions their mother. She may have no longer been living, as is portrayed in this *Bold Girls* story, but that is pure fiction. She may have been living at the time these events occurred.

Philip was an important figure in early church events. He was the first evangelist to the outcast population known as the Samaritans, with whom he performed miracles and baptized both men and women (Acts 8:4–13). He also taught the Ethiopian eunuch in the well-known story of Acts. 8:26–39. Philip looked past cultural and racial differences, and accepted all people as being capable of believing in Jesus. This calling to evangelize to populations outside the circles of traditional Judaism was no doubt taught to his daughters by his example.

The connection in the story between Philip's daughters with Paul's nephew is a totally fictional invention in this *Bold Girls* story. But then again, something like this story could be possible (Acts 23:16). The truth is, nothing is known about Paul's sister and her son except for the verse that tells us that the young man alerted Paul's guards about imminent danger to Paul. His motivation for aiding Paul, and how he came to this information, is entirely speculation in this *Bold Girls* story. We can be certain that this was a risky thing to do. Did he act purely out of concern for a relative;

The Daughters Who Prophesied

did he have admiration for his mother's brother; did he believe in Paul's cause for Christ? We cannot say for certain, but these motivations would also make for an interesting story. God is working his wonders through the actions of young people. Both boys and girls have their place in furthering the gospel!

QUESTIONS FOR DISCUSSION

1. Review the life of Paul, his missionary journeys, and his means of travel. What difference did he make in the spread of Christianity? What books of the Bible did he write?

2. This *Bold Girls* story is another example of girls living as minorities within a majority culture that is not friendly to their way of life. Is this your experience where you live? Is it important that you practice and remember the language and culture of your parents and grandparents, or should you put your heritage behind you and learn the ways of a new country?

3. How do you think you are gifted to work in your church and in the community? Are you limited in what you do by your age or gender? Should this be so? Is there any indication in the Bible that the Spirit will gift individuals according to gender, nationality, or economic status?

4. What evidence is in the New Testament for women as prophets? In the New Testament, look up Luke 2:36–38; Acts 21:8–9; 1 Corinthians 11:4–5. In the Old Testament, look up 2 Kings 22:14.

5. Who was Stephen? What is his connection to Philip?

RELATED CULTURAL AND HISTORICAL QUESTIONS TO EXPLORE

1. In this *Bold Girls* story, the sisters are engaged in copying texts. This is purely a fictional addition, but it could have been possible. In the days before printing presses, how could the letters of Paul be transmitted to new readers? Who did the copying in the first century and in the later centuries? What materials did they use and what did the books look like?

2. The ancient culture of the Greeks and Romans in the first century is very interesting. Draw a timeline of major events. What was life like for young people at that time? For women and girls? Who were the emperors and other famous people of first-century Roman history? Have people learned from history or are they still making the same mistakes?

3. What were the issues that separated Christianity from Judaism? What do the two religions have in common, and what are the differences?

4. Can you imagine your future as either a married person or a single person? Can you accept either of these choices as an exciting possibility for furthering the work of Jesus? What are the advantages and disadvantages of either alternative, and how will you decide for yourself?

5. What does the following Bible verse mean to you, and how should it impact how we live? "There is neither Jew nor Greek, there is neither slave nor free, there is neither male nor female; for you are all one in Christ Jesus" (Galatians 3:28).

SUGGESTED TOPICS OF DISCUSSION FOR TEACHERS AND PARENTS OF OLDER STUDENTS

1. What is your conclusion concerning spiritual gifts such as speaking in tongues, prophecy, and healing? Do these gifts still exist today, or were they only practiced during biblical times?

2. Why do some churches practice infant baptism and others wait until the children are old enough to make their own confessions?

3. This story presents a good opening for a discussion of circumcision. Why was circumcision replaced with baptism? What are the differences?

4. The Jerusalem Council (Acts 15) prohibited certain activities for both Christian Jews and Gentiles. These prohibitions included not eating blood, strangled animals, or foods offered to idols. Sexual immorality was also prohibited. Why are some of these commands retained in the church today, and why are they particularly important?

Lesson Plan Ideas

THE FOLLOWING ACTIVITIES AND ideas are designed to help students gain a better biblical-historical context for the *Bold Girls* stories. Teachers can use these activities to help students preview the biblical world of a *Bold Girls* story. Conversely, students can engage in these activities after reading a *Bold Girls* story to better understand the people, places, and events that were depicted.

1. On a large map of the Middle East, find the location of each *Bold Girls* story. Use this matching exercise to get started. Note that, in some cases, the girls moved from one country to another. Can we visit these places today?

2. Draw a timeline either on a classroom whiteboard, bulletin board, or your notebook paper. Graph paper is ideal. Starting with 1400 bc, mark off 100 year increments until ad 100. Find the approximate years when each *Bold Girls* story takes place.

3. Make a list of all the books of the Bible, from Genesis to Revelation. Find the book in the Bible where each *Bold Girls* story is found. Who is the author of each of these biblical books?

4. Using the timeline created in activity 2, note other places and events in the world beyond the Bible during these years. Who were the important kings, what were some of the most important events, and which nations were the strongest?

5. What would the *Bold Girls* wear in each of these settings? How does that change, depending on the country, climate, time of year, their activities, or their economic status? Students in a class could dress as one of the *Bold Girls* and then have the class guess which *Bold Girl* they represent.

Lesson Plan Ideas

6. The *Bold Girls* are involved in many different activities. What would be the daily activities of a particular bold girl in a given story? Students can pantomime the different activities for the rest of the class, and students can use those clues to guess which *Bold Girl* is being depicted. How are the activities of these girls different from those of the girls in our time and place?

7. Look up books about foods of the Holy Land or recipes from the Bible. As a bold girl, what foods would you eat? How would that food be produced and prepared? Who would prepare the food? What would each person do during the various stages of preparation?

8. Draw pictures of the *Bold Girls* or make illustrations for the stories.

9. Find books about ancient Greece, Rome, Egypt, and Holy Lands. Look for illustrations and information about daily life in those times and places.

10. For each of the *Bold Girls*, determine the identity of her other family members. Look for hints in the original passage from the Bible. Build on information available from the Bible, but remember that the *Bold Girls* stories are mostly fictional.

Matching Quiz

1. Jerusalem: The home of Mary Mark
2. Caesarea
3. Egypt
4. Jerusalem: Quarters of Zadok
5. Damascus
6. Capernaum
7. Jerusalem: Palace of Caiaphas
8. Philippi (Greece)
9. Sinai
10. Jerusalem: Walls

A. The Girl Whose Hand Jesus Touched
B. The Maids Who Questioned
C. The Girl Who Found Her Own Voice
D. The Daughters Who Prophesied
E. Rhoda, the Servant Girl Who Persisted
F. The Daughters Who Built the Walls of Jerusalem
G. Miriam Who Negotiated
H. The Girl Who Spied
I. Five Sisters Who Asked for Their Inheritance
J. The Servant Girl Who Boldly Witnessed

Answers: 1. E. 2. D. 3. G. 4. H. 5. J. 6. A. 7. B. 8. C. 9. I. 10. F.

Quiz Your Knowledge of *Bold Girls Speak*

1. Does the Bible ever indicate that women inherited property?

    Yes, the daughters of Zelophehad in Numbers 27:5; and the daughters of Job in Job 42:15; Achsah, the daughter of Caleb in Joshua 15:16–19

2. Who bravely approached the daughter of a powerful monarch?

    Miriam, in Exodus 2:7.

3. Name a woman in the Bible who we meet both as a child and an adult?

    Miriam, assuming the sister in Exodus 2:4 is Miriam.

4. Whose daughters in Jerusalem used nontraditional skills for girls?

    The daughters of Shallum who repaired the walls of Jerusalem in Nehemiah 3:12.

5. Who was the *Bold Girl* who witnessed to an enemy soldier?

    An unnamed servant girl of Naaman in 2 Kings 5.

6. Who was entrusted with carrying an important message?

    An unnamed servant girl in 2 Samuel 17:17.

7. Which *Bold Girl* is possibly named after her place of origin?

    Rhoda in Acts 12:5:7.

8. Which *Bold Girls* are given spoken words that are recorded in the Bible?

    Miriam in Exodus 2:7; servant of Naaman in 2 Kings 5:3; servant girls in the house of Caiaphas in Matthew 26:69–71; Rhoda in Acts 12:14; unnamed servant girl in Philippi, Acts 16:17.

9. Which *Bold Girls* are actually named in the Bible?

    A sister of the baby is introduced in Exodus 2:4 and is not named in the passage, but traditionally this sister has been connected with Miriam; the daughters of Zelophehad in Numbers 27:1; Rhoda in Acts 12:13.

10. Which *Bold Girls* had contact with Peter?

    The servants of Caiaphas in Matthew 26:69; Rhoda in Acts 12:5–17.

The Maids Who Questioned

STAGE PLAY VERSION

Stage: Stone wall on left and right. Gate in the wall at stage right. Stage left a tree. In the middle a fire pit. A bench against the wall stage left. Back drop has a painting of a large two-story stone palace with functioning door in the middle. Windows are cut out and covered with a translucent fabric screen. Lamps behind so they can be later lit and shadows formed behind.

Characters:
  Abby: Serious girl, believes in Jesus.
  Liz: Fun-loving, skeptical about Jesus.
  Aaron: Doesn't believe in Jesus. Aaron and Liz like each other.
  Joe: Believes in Jesus. Interested in Abby.
  Simon: Knowledgeable, undecided.
  3–5 Important looking priests
  Soldier 1, Soldier 2, Soldier 3, Soldier 4
  More nonspeaking soldiers and priests as available
  Peter: Mature man, moody, deeply disturbed.
  Jesus: (Non-speaking part.)

SCENE ONE

Abby, Liz, Aaron, Joe, and Simon are doing work in the courtyard. Liz is sweeping, Joe walks on stage carrying a basket of charcoal and then starts to

Stage Play Version

prepare the fire. The other three are doing some kind of household or garden tasks.

Abby: This Jesus of Nazareth, do you think he is the promised Messiah, the son of David?

Liz: *(Jabbing her broom into the ground)* No way, he is a rabble rouser, he preaches insurrection! Master Caiaphas says that if Jesus is allowed to continue teaching in the Temple, a riot will start. Then the Roman soldiers will move in and there will be plenty of trouble.

Aaron: You bet; you should have been there the other day in the temple. He just kicked over the tables of the merchants who were selling doves for the sacrifices. Tempers were rising and angry words echoed throughout the temple walls. Feathers and coins flew everywhere. Who does he think he is to disturb the peace in this way?

Simon: *(Leaning against the old olive tree)* Annas and Caiaphas looked plenty hot under their itchy beards on that day. Our masters are the chief priests of the Sanhedrin and are responsible to maintain order in the temple. Now, with crowds of the country people coming into Jerusalem for Passover, they have to be sure there is no trouble. Those backward village fishermen from Galilee, they are so easily swayed.

Joe: *(Setting down a basket of charcoal)* Jesus is not a violent man at all. I saw him entering Jerusalem on the Sabbath past, riding a donkey. The crowds were cheering him with songs, 'Hosanna in the highest . . . Peace in heaven and glory in the highest!' They were waving palms and laying their coats on his path. He was the most gentle man you could imagine, but his eyes were so sad.

Sudden crackling sounds like branches breaking. The actors all look up. Leaves and twigs fall on the stage to appear like they are falling from the tree. Chicken sounds. A stuffed chicken falls on the ground in front of them and is pulled off the stage by a string. Aaron takes a few steps toward the chicken to appear to try to catch it.

The Maids Who Questioned

Liz: (*To Aaron*) That old rooster again; didn't you get him for the Passover dinner? I thought the cook wanted a good fat chicken for the stew.

Aaron: That bird is even tougher than you! You would have to stand by the fire a week to cook him tender in the pot.

Liz: Well then, I hope he keeps waking you up nights with his crowing outside your loft. He seems to be attracted to guys who talk too much!

Abby: There will be a lot of guests in the house for Passover. We are going to need every bird and lamb in the yard to feed all the men that have come through the gate this afternoon. Many of them are the chief priests and scribes that I recognize from my many errands to the temple area. They really seem to be preoccupied, not in the mood for any celebration.

Simon: It's that Jesus fellow. I spied Pontius Pilate approaching the palace this morning with a group of Roman soldiers. You can be sure that when the governor comes to Jerusalem something is going on. There are rumors of a trial.

Abby: What can they try him for? Jesus has healed people that are lame and driven away evil spirits. Everyone is talking about how he raised Lazarus from the grave. He teaches forgiveness and love. I would like to learn more about him.

Aaron: Don't forget, he heals on the Sabbath! That is clearly breaking the law. What will he try to do next? It has been one absurd thing after the other!

Insistent knocking at the gate interrupts the argument. All the servants stand straight and pick up their items to leave. Abby smoothes her clothes and moves to stage right toward the gate.

Aaron: (*To Liz as he moves to stage left*) Now Liz, be sure to keep that courtyard swept up so these high and mighty visitors don't step in dirt and get their sandals soiled.

Liz: *(Follows after Aaron and swats his behind with the broom as they leave the stage)*
You get that rooster or you are going to be in it up to your neck.

Abby: *(Bowing)* Come in, most esteemed visitors; Master Caiaphas is expecting you upstairs in the palace.

Three or more important looking men enter through the gate stage right and barely look at Abby. They proceed with loud steps to the door of the house. They open the door and enter the house. Shut the door.

SCENE TWO

Abby: *(Alone on the stage looking around, then she starts to light the fire)*
Thank goodness the yard is clean. I have to be careful who I let into the gate. So far I have recognized everyone. Very fortunate I have a memory for faces. It is true what they say, that the servants of Caiaphas get around. There is a good reason that the house of Caiaphas is known as a place of intrigue and whisperings. Yes, the face of Jesus was remarkable when I saw him. Not that he was a handsome man, it was more what he said and his manner of speaking . . .

Liz: *(Sneaking up behind her)* You were speaking of a handsome man?

Abby: *(Startled)* You have only one thing on your mind, Liz. Honestly, some beauty is more than skin deep. I was thinking of Jesus. What I have heard about him is very convincing. What if he is the promised Messiah our Jewish nation has longed for since the days of Isaiah?

Liz: Messiah or not, I have been eavesdropping under the window and overhearing the arguments going on all evening in the upper chamber. I have never seen the household so tense. It is going to be a very long night, and we will have to keep the fire going.

Some time passes; the fire is lit. The stage gets darker like it is evening.

SCENE THREE

Stage right the gate swings open with sudden noise. A crowd of soldiers burst in with shouting. Carrying torches. Some are dressed in Roman armor. They move toward the house. They are half dragging a man between them.

Abby: *(Abby and Liz have moved to the front of the stage)* They didn't even announce themselves. How do we know who has entered?

They both turn and stare at the man being dragged from stage right to the middle of the back stage.

Liz: Isn't that the Jesus of Nazareth you were speaking of?

Abby: It can't be . . . but it seems to be so. How horrible! How can they be so cruel to someone who has been so kind?

The boys join the girls, and they all huddle together turned toward the house. They look afraid. Joe put his arm around Abby. The lights behind the windows turn on. Shadows are seen in the windows. Unintelligible shouts from the house.

Joe: Tonight will be a night not soon forgotten.

SCENE FOUR

The men dressed as Roman soldiers come back on stage through the house door. They sit down around the fire like they own the place. They warm their hands and make themselves comfortable like they are going to stay awhile. The servants stand in the shadows nearby.

Soldier 1: Can you believe the audacious behavior of one of those disciples! This dude went and sliced his ear off . . . what's that guy's name? . . . yeah, Malchus . . . cut his ear right off . . . whack . . . with the huge sword. Like he was going to be some big hero or something . . . to think that was going to scare us away!

Stage Play Version

The soldiers slap their thighs and laugh.

Soldier 2: Oh yeah, I was shaking in my sandals . . . like this. (*Makes a mocking imitation with his knees knocking together*)

Joe: (*To Simon; they are standing together stage left*) Hey, we know Malchus. He's one of the older servants, actually my cousin, here in the household, and a personal guard of Caiaphas.

Soldier 3: Healed him, just like that. (*Snaps his fingers*)

Soldier 4: Yeah, I saw it too! This guy, Jesus, just touched his ear and it was reattached; it was a miracle. Hey, where is this fella, Malchus? Would I like to talk to him! Must have went inside. What is going on up there in the house?

Soldier 1: So who is this motley soul, Jesus, we arrested tonight? Some kind of healing! There has to be some kind of magic trick.

Soldier 2: Imagine, under arrest, his own disciples are trying to help him, and he goes and heals the enemy. Like whose side is he on, man?

Soldier 3: "For all who take the sword will perish by the sword." Those are his exact words.

The servants huddle just within earshot, glance nervously at each other, scarcely believing their ears. Unnoticed, a man has come on stage left and is sitting on the bench. The stage gets quiet, the soldiers continue their conversation and antics, but now in mime.

SCENE FIVE

Liz on stage right notices the solitary man, elbows Abby and points.

Liz: (*Loud stage whisper*) Hey Abby, did you let that guy in? Who is he? Did he come in with the soldiers?

The Maids Who Questioned

Abby: I don't know, I think he is okay. I recognize him as a follower of Jesus.

Liz: You are too trusting; now go find out for sure. *(Liz pushes her in that direction)*
We need to know who is in here or we could be in big trouble.

Abby: Does it have to be me? Well, if he is one of the followers of Jesus, maybe I can find out something.

The other servants watch out of the corners of their eyes as Abby approaches the withdrawn figure.

Abby: Sir, I need to ask. You are not also one of this man's disciples, are you?

Peter: *(Abruptly)* I do not know nor understand what you are talking about.

He then exits to stage left with haste.

Sound of rooster crowing.

Aaron: *(Looks up into the tree)* There goes that rooster again. Of course with all the activity and light around here, even though it must be well past midnight, the dumb bird probably thinks it is daytime. *(The other servants look at him and moan at his bad joke)*

The soldiers keep up their discussion around the fire. The talking stops every time the roar of voices is heard from the house. Then they all look at the house.

Abby: Whatever could be going on? I do hope they at least give Jesus a fair chance.

Joe: Oh, I am very afraid that Caiaphas, Annas, and the other big shots have their minds already made up about Jesus.

Simon: I heard him say, "Better to have one person die for the people, than have many perish." We are going to have riots here if something isn't done quickly.

Stage Play Version

Peter comes back on stage, sits on stool at stage left unnoticed.

Abby: But Jesus is not the one getting the people all riled up. If the authorities would just really listen to him. He is talking about another, eternal kingdom. I am convinced he is an innocent man.

Aaron: Hey, there's that guy again.

Abby: Someone else go up to him. I don't think he is up to any good. Liz, your turn; see what you can find out.

Liz: No way; he seems to be in a foul mood. Come with me. All right, I'll just shout from here. *(She turns toward Peter)* Hey you, surely you are with Jesus; you talk like a Galilean!

Peter: I swear, I do not know what you are talking about! *(Additional profanities, and he abruptly walks off the stage)*

Sound of rooster crowing.

Simon: Whoo! And I thought we got earthy once in a while.

Abby: He does seem like something is weighing very heavily on his conscience. He is a troubled man. No doubt he is very concerned about Jesus.

A roar of voices from the window above. Everyone in the courtyard looks up at lighted windows.

Voice from backstage: You have heard his blasphemy!

Joe: That is Caiaphas; I know it is him.

Voices from backstage: Death to him! Death to Jesus!
Peter has come quietly back on stage and sits on a stool against the wall stage left.

The group of servants stand together.

The Maids Who Questioned

The soldiers stand in another huddled group.

Abby dabs her eyes with back of her hand and starts to pray silently.

Aaron shrugs his shoulders and tries to warm his arms.

Liz sighs and stares blankly straight ahead.

Simon looks down and shuffles his feet in the dust.

Joe cinches his fist. He sees the Galilean man standing by himself. Abby catches his eye and nods.

Joe: Certainly you are one of the Galileans; your accent gives you away.

Peter: *(Shouting, knocking over the stool)* I do not know the man!

Rooster crows.

Peter stumbles off stage to left, barely staying on his feet.

From backstage: *Sound of loud sobbing.*

Liz: That man is beyond all help.

The house door flings open with a crash. A rush of shoving men spills out of the house.

The servants retreat to each side of the stage.

The guards grab their gear, which is strewn around the dying fire.

The men from the house shove each other through the courtyard, making their way to the gate.

With his hands bound, held upright between two guards, is Jesus, obviously beaten, barely walking.

Abby: He has the weight of the world on his shoulders. There is something more going on here . . . if I weren't so helpless . . . God help Jesus!

The guards scramble after the priest leaving the house and exit through gate stage right. They leave the gate standing open.

The sound of a crowd gets softer.

The stage lightens with a pink glow over the house on the back wall.

A silhouette of a rooster sits on top of the house.

Aaron, Liz, and Simon leave the stage left slowly.

Abby and Joe stare through the opened gate as though looking at the people who just left stage right.

Last faint sounds of crowd retreating into the distance.

Abby and Joe: *(Together)* What will this day bring?

www.ingramcontent.com/pod-product-compliance
Lightning Source LLC
Chambersburg PA
CBHW052102230426
43662CB00036B/1765